Illinois Central College
Learning Resources Center

SPRING SHADE

Poems · 1931–1970

SPRING SHADE
Poems · 1931-1970

ROBERT
FITZGERALD, 1910 -

A NEW DIRECTIONS BOOK

P S
3 5 I I
. I 9 2 2
∧
5 6

ACKNOWLEDGMENTS

"Chorus" from *Oedipus Rex* reprinted by permission of the publishers of *Oedipus Rex,* translated by Dudley Fitts and Robert Fitzgerald, copyright 1949 by Harcourt Brace Jovanovitch, Inc. Robert Fitzgerald's translations of "The Narcissus Cantata" by Valéry and *Chronique* by St.-John Perse are reprinted by permission of Princeton University Press. *The Collected Works of Paul Valéry,* Vol. 3, Jackson Mathews, ed., Bollingen Series XLV; copyright © 1960 by Bollingen Foundation. St.-John Perse, *Chronique,* Bollingen Series LXIX; copyright © 1961 by Bollingen Foundation. The translation of Borges's "Love's Priority" is reprinted from *An Anthology of Contemporary Latin-American Poetry,* Dudley Fitts, ed.; copyright 1942, 1945 by New Directions Publishing Corporation.

The following poems first appeared in *The New Yorker:* "Mise en Scene," "The Queens," "Errantry," "Lightness in Autumn," "Jesu, Joy of Man's Desiring," "July in Indiana," "Epiphany," "Patrum Propositum" and "Aerial." These first appeared in *Poetry:* "Physis," "Figlio Maggiore" and "Metaphysical."

Other poems were first published in these magazines: *Encounter, Fire Exit, The Harvard Advocate, The Hudson Review, The Kenyon Review, The London Tablet, The Malahat Review, The Nation, New York Review of Books, Partisan Review,* and *Ski.* The poem "Dudley Fitts" first appeared in *The Boston Globe.*

First published clothbound and as ND Paperbook 311 in 1971
Published simultaneously in Canada by McClelland & Stewart, Ltd.
Manufactured in the United States of America

New Directions Books are published for James Laughlin
by New Directions Publishing Corporation,
333 Sixth Avenue, New York 10014

CONTENTS

POEMS · 1931–1935

for Dudley Fitts

WINTER NIGHT

THE GREY day left the dusk in doubt.
Now it is dark.
Nightfall and no stars are out,
But this black wind will set its mark
Like anger on the souls that stir
From chimney side or sepulcher.

From hill to pasture moans the snow.
The farms hug tight
Their shaking ribs against the blow.
There is no mercy in this night
Nor scruple to its wrath. The dead
Sleep light this wind being overhead.

SONG AFTER CAMPION

Ravished lute, sing to her virgin ears,
Soft notes thy strings repeating;
Plucked harp, whose amorous song she hears,
Tell her the time is fleeting;
Night-tide and my distress of love
O speak, sweet numbers,
That pity her heart may move
Before she slumbers.

Pale moth, that from the moon doth fly,
Fickle enchantments weaving,
Night faery, come my lady nigh
When the rich masques are leaving;
Tell her who lieth still alone
Love is a treasure
Fair as the frail lute's tone
And perished measure.

CHARLES RIVER NOCTURNE

Reflecting remote swords, chilled in the calm
And liquid darkness, lights on the esplanade
Prolong the night's edge downward all night long

To those whose nostrils ache with the strong darkness

Those who in hunger press against the waters,

Those without birth or death, to whom the cold
Ocean long laboring in her regal womb
Whispers a word of foam.

              The lavish cars
Move westward in an eddy and dance of shadow
Under the dazed lamps on the lifeless shore.

NIGHT SONG

ANGUISH and delight are now
Coiled in darkness on the bough,
And iron time deflowers spring
Secretly, the secret thing.
Mind and body, as they must,
Invent a terminus to lust,
Preserving the despair they make . . .
Pray the Lord my soul to take.

When this incontinent despair
Turns sick with love in sunless air,
A firmer bed than bed of stone
Take up my cast of flesh and bone,
A sharper song than rue or willow
Weep me dead upon my pillow:
I who strangled life with sleep . . .
Pray the Lord my soul to keep.

NIGHT IMAGES

LATE in the cold night wakened, and heard wind,
And lay with eyes closed and silent, knowing
These words how bodiless they are, this darkness
Empty under my roof and the panes rattling
Roughed by wind. And so lay and imagined
Somewhere far off black seas heavy-shouldered
Plunging on sand and the ebb off-streaming and
Thunder forever. So lying bethought me, friend,
What traffic ghouls have, or this be legend,
In low inland hollows of the earth, under
Shade of moon, the night moaning, and bitter frost;
And feared the riches of my bones, long given
Into this earth, should tumble to their hands.
No girl or ghost beside me, and I lonely,
Remembering gardens, lilac scent, or twilight
Descending late in summer on that town,
I lay and found my years departed from me,
And feared the cold bed and the wind, absurdly
Alone with silence and the trick of tears.

THRENOS

ALWAYS before the rain comes before the windows
darkening in our house lengthen upon us
between the time of reverence and withdrawal
a clock's exquisite hands repose and wait

The suitors stirring in the hall sorrowful
tell of dead kings here is Odysseus dead

graven his bones and garments Sir I pray you
sleep in your vast dwelling sleep or sing now
cool voice cut in motion of the whole wind
sing no one will answer you the leaf invisible
falls on the tile the watchman sighs in the street

Always before the rain comes and the darkness
across the islands here in this granite light
holds the frail surface of the world together

here is Odysseus dead here is the night

OFFICE FOR EASTER

THE ROBINS claim the spring
And I say of the dead, they are holy.
I revere them in their anger,
Their sins. I say they are holy.

The streetcar's sad bell
Reawakens their love:
Forsythia, yellow leaves,
Or new slender laurel.

Late in a southern town —
The pure sun in the grass —
I heard my mother's song
On the stair of a strange house.

Then all the rooms were light
And warm, the wind falling.
I could not hear her pain.
My cigarette burned down.

This I make bloom for her
As spring in her country.

PHRASE

Sorrowful love passes from transparencies
to transparencies of bitter starlight
between antiquities and antiquities so simply

as in evening a soft bird flies down
and rests on a white railing under leaves

Love thinks in this quietness of falling
leaves birds or rain from the hushes
of summer clouds through luminous centuries

Touch unconsolable love the hands of your ancestors

MIDSUMMER

THE ADOLESCENT night, breath of the town,
Porchswings and whispers, maple leaves unseen
Deploying moonlight quieter than a man dead
After the locust's song. These homes were mine
And are not now forever, these on the steps
Children I think removed to many places,
Lost among hushed years, and so strangely known.

This business is well ended. If in the dark
The firefly made his gleam and sank therefrom,
Yet someone's hand would have him, the wet grass
Bed him no more. From corners of the lawn
The dusk-white dresses flutter and are past.
Before our bed time there were things to say,
Remembering tree-bark, crickets, and the first star . . .

After, and as the sullenness of time
Went on from summer, here in a land alien
Made I my perfect fears and flower of thought:
Sleep being no longer swift in the arms of pain,
Revisitations are convenient with a cough,
And there is something I would say again
If I had not forever, if there were time.

BEFORE HARVEST

DEEP and soft and far off over country
A train whistle is explaining something strange
To the cool night, so long, sweet, far away.

In your dark rooms under the elm branches,
Stir, O sleepers in the country towns,
Auburn, Divernon, Chatham, Jacksonville . . .
This is the ebb and weary hour of night.

Only a child benumbed with dreaming
Wakes and listens to the visiting rain
Lick its tongues in the leaves and pass away.

HIMEROS

THE LOCUST sobs in the leaves. Her dusty hair
My love has now let fall upon the sun's
Stream. Beyond pale trestles
Flows evening: darkness and earth-drift.
Under a shard of moon the locust sings,
Mourning holocausts of summer.

Centaurs in warm forests wheel silently
Over leaf-mould, where the huntress
Walks with stiff breasts.
A star at the bedside clinks.
At last knee to knee we say, Peace —
Though in the air of bats a clown listens.

Our present death, dear time, of all purity
Takes lordly revenue in this twilight,
The leaf-veined delta of the spreading year.
The field is silted for the richer harvest,
Crystalline shores regained
And a slow surf beating our nets forever.

SONG FOR SEPTEMBER

RESPECT the dreams of old men, said the cricket,
Summer behind the song, the streams falling
Ledge to ledge in the mountains where clouds come.
Attend the old men who wander
Daylight and evening in the air grown cold,
Time thins, leaving their will to wind and whispers;
The bells are swallowed gently under ground.

Because in time the birds will leave this country,
Waning south, not to return again;
Because we walk in gardens among grasses,
Touching the garments of the wind that passes,
Dimming our eyes —

Give benches to the old men, said the cricket,
Listening by cool ways to the world that dies
Fainter than seas drawn off from mist and stone.
The rain that speaks at night is the prayer's answer.
What are dry phantoms to the old men
Lying at night alone?

They are not here whose gestures we have known,
Their hands in the dusk, their frail hair in the sun.

ELEGY

WHAT should you know at last when spirit's
Spun from you, bobbin of bone, ghostbody in the sun?
Enumerate your keen, wind-feathered
Moods up-tossed and patterned in swift weather
With colors of skirts and flowers;

And those more constant images that serve
To guide the blinded time: the scent of sickness
Over blankets in a cold room, the shades drawn
At evening, rosaries told years ago
By mild hands motionless or moving
Wisely in soft light, and the strange house in spring
With dust under the canvas bellies of the chairs,
The new screens painted and the flowering wind . . .

You are grown old to be thus disembodied
By a few dreams pulled gently, and would be
Thinned out of mind if I should sever in you
The nervous strand of sorrow. God be with you;
When I have touched this only I shall leave you,
And walk very gladly and quietly out of doors,
My trousers rustling round my legs like leaves
In the slow autumn air, the still fountains.

FOR THE OTHERS

THEY will come to my house, to the street's end
In the tedious season,
Naming the dry leaf and the wind at morning
Bearing death.

From the well cut helm and craft of speech,
Let me turn clearly
To grip in daylight time's still edge,
Finding my body, sight, touch, hearing, strange.
Identity then with what mind in what place
Of all that make the story?

                    Birds
Sing in the dark trees at the world's end
In the evening of time. The bearded men
Stand there among the horses. Musicians play.

And there are valleys in the mountains
And women cutting the hay, and carrying it
In under warm rain.

                 These we know.

O father, father
These many days and many harvests
We endured, and the grey sea under mists,
The agony of our daughters, and
Old men dying in candlelight
With summer's passage —

                       remembering

Landfalls, delay of autumn, grief among dreams.

THE WOMEN bow and flutter in the field.
The grain lies white with wind in the wide shadow.
Summer is dark, as in the ancient time.

This fair cloud that blooms in the northwest
Has darkened now, as in the ancient time,
And clouds are still at dawn on the soft mountains.

Husks after harvest we shall leave for rain
And our heels' trace in the loam:
The stir of boughs has warned us,
Fruit in the grass reminds us . . .

I. We made this journey not in desire
But thirst. When we entered the towns
In the smoky light, the whistles, and the lanterns
Swinging or still beside the shunted cars,
It was not love we took to brood upon.
There were foes in our legends, whom alone
We fought, breath vowed to their meaning.
By various paths and twilights, corners of rain,
Watching the children play, lamplighters come,
We stayed to hear their dangerous low voices.

Saying when the wind had fallen: Sorrow.
Eyes are filled with death. The rooms are
Hives of evil. Dustclouds on the road
Follow the traveler like a malediction.
By night the leaves are years
And distant each one in that silvered dark.

Or marvels stretched there in the stillness:
Gleam of the wolf among the alders, beasts
Fawning on stairhead, door-whine in the night,
Or mothers risen infamous from the grave.

And one would come in sleep, which was the vampire
In under light, boundless, whose near brow
Turned the glad fiend's with sudden clasp or sigh;
And others in that slow time beyond terror —
Madmen in armies trampling the vast brain,
Gnashing as engines quietly, or cold
In the void ether, visions
Famished through interminable dark,
Which wakened us our bodies, the strange bones
Trembling in single wonder of themselves.

II. And in the sun where we were friends and strangers,
Kicking tough oars together clean of the foam,
We knew we were alone upon that water;
Or on long fields in a leaf-blowing autumn,
Handling the hard ball backward through the sunlight,
Lonely under the high kick, toward the tackle
Thrown and the curt cleats taking us and down, the
Bitter turf our vision, so alone there
Waiting for pain in the numb fracture, listened.

Handshake and smiling, or the rainy crowds
In cities glistening with the tick of cabs,
Or sunlight crossing the loud corners, left us
Always to question a still room ourselves:

When winter lifted her cool beams
Dawnwide and whitened in the ache of light,
The grey mask on the pillow turned, death issued
Pure from our lips as from a studying child,
Till waking tendons netted us alive.

Head reared into the morning.

And in cold mirrors our deep eyes,
Familiars of starlight, curious
Interpreters of the sun, the fire and clear
Waterlights of noon upon our walls:
Webs for the spring of shadow.
                              Where have you been?
What have you noticed? What have you hidden? Who
Speaks to you in this one's voice? Still there?
So hurt, so sorry, so angry, so ashamed . . .

III. Girls came with their wide eyes, the faint flames
Branching about them, and their flowerlike hair:
Avid, delicate harlots: those pale ones
Received us in stately dream, in daylight were
Beloved, their warm breasts and beautiful shoulders
Sweet comforts which the lutanist sang of old.
A long walk after. The fat bawds of smoke
Impaled on phalloi in a pantomime
Wriggled a squealing answer to our love.

And hatred rotting with pity in our houses
Filmed, a thin gum for eyelids over midnight.
We sat on our two bones and we were blind.

Unless a far light, home light, the old vision,
Land of children, loveliest in the west,
Glowed in the time-drift
Small as a minuet-whisper and as dear.
And our hearts faint with grief to think of it:
How crickets dinned in the sure evening, late
Locusts would come, each to his ancient tree;
Mowers on many lawns, leveling summer,
Measured the slow festival of the air;

Or in bright gusts of winter by the door,
The shadows thin beneath a glitter of icicles,
Our mothers in their ceremonial furs,
Delicious ladies laughing, their cheeks cold —
Gone from the light like their breath's vapor, leaving
This image or another bound in thought
With scent of old spoons, handkerchiefs and roses.

Time that brought them to their narrow anguish
Removed us from their rooms.

IV.   Lamplight and dark,
The many years and splendor. We were those men
Who saw from dunes on the dark ocean,
On windy earth, the wasteful magnificent seasons
Driving their clouds, as planet tilted turning
Radiance toward the poles. Inland were forests
Kept the snow in winter, shade in summer;
Plains were a long gaze and a sigh from hills.

We moved there always in the northern weather,

Briefly together or alone,
Heard the flush of motors, cylinder flutter
Under us, the fiery power sound
Swelling the road backward. Against glass
Wind blustered brightening from the simple farms,
And there were black fields and the plowman, lonely,
Inching through the sunlit treasure of distance,
And starlings rising in stillness on meadowlands.

Or walked upon an aerodrome in our dream
Below the downward hush and remorse of engines,
Their wings sighing home.
Blades chuckered and a harsh roar kicked up dust:
Swung to the wind and traveled. Dreaming we saw
Bright fields and sun, bright garlands flung from struts,
The land tilt in the long air, the shrunken land
Drift down to southward at a cloud's pace:

And came in a bower of loneliness and cloud,
Riding with dark engines depth of wind,
Where cities smouldering in a nick of rivers shone,
Dud fireworks by their runnels, glittered in mist.
Sea lay, quicksilver, eastward, and a sail
Perched like the white pinch of a butterfly . . .

Over the dials our enormous hands . . .

V. We wakened in the clear light of the mountains,
In white rooms of the valley people, breathing
Under their curtains icy air. We swam

In black streams running with a foam upon them,
Or stood in that high summer with the quiet
Presence of those we loved. In winter, skiing.
Our faint years fell like snow beyond the valleys.
And over them a cross bore blackened Christ
Against the snowfields like a scarecrow.

                                              There
Cars were steaming in that gash of light,
Nose over pass to cloudland and deep plain,
As those of Lombardy or Piedmont, burning
Southward, the low wind in the ilex rustling
Memoried evening and the cypress shades:

Or then by northern rivers under towers
Graven in purest sky, with sometimes bells
Remembered in the nerves of many dead —
In their streets wandered, listening to the flutist
        who loved
His single note, sweet in the russet shuffle
Of fall, his bound throat bent to the measure,
Or slowly in the evening dust and gold
On grey stones pausing, listened . . . So from the vine,
The window bar and the cold garden eaves,
Haled by a décor of heads turning there:
Such courtesy, not gross enough for time . . .

VI. At night above the embers of those towns
Coiled with thin-running lights and girls' laughter,
We heard sea-music and the slap of seas;
Odysseus, our father, wanderer;

Or Anchises, to whom the Cyprian came,
The figure tall, with cool thighs in the light,
Unkindly glory from the islands,
Linking before her the rich padding cats,
When in her temple the wind lifted
First at twilight round the columns, flowering
Formal leaves yet softer than the loved myrtle
Above the shy sandals, shadowed dance ...

And in young frosty mornings, breathing down,
We knelt with our wet brows under the flames
That burned nightlong, silent and merciful.
Airs from the fragrant stone, the great cathedral
Organs raging, Holy, Holy, Holy,
And their sad liturgies like incense rising
Far off on a low violet imagined land.

There where small leaves turned grey after the wind,
Dove-bearing, over mild dust we saw them come
Slowly in weariness, his followers,
Walking by Olivet in the moon's hours:
In their eyes were narratives and wisdom,
Sweetened by an old light in the cedars;
Their polished hands held fast the ancient staves;
They were sere and kind to the children of women;
Their feet were sensible of stones and leaves,
And in evening they could write on the papyrus
Legends of their lord Christ: they were strange men.

And stranger light than theirs, a stranger time,
The child caught in the glass: unhistoried years

When Bluebeard throve, who knew what dainty dread
Would take his milkwhite staring ladies,
Their cold hands timid on the strings —

So hallowed that flood of western air and pale
Where no leaf burned but sundown in his hall,
The sweet world, God's world, marvelous with fear . . .

VII. And we who dreamed these things came down
Stair after stair, rim within rim of darkness,
To enter in our hunger the hell of cities,
Torn by crowds, their faces blowing skyward
Under the flares and premonition of rifles:
The presses humming on the looms of night,
And news-sheets crumpled, howling in an alley
Of evil rising in the shade of war,
Such evil as in our time lived under us
Dissolving shining things . . . dissolving
The young men on their benches into death.

At length to make our verse for oblivious winter
In the late night of nuns and mounted police,
Old nuns who pray in the cold rooms of the sick
For intercession of Mary at their hour of death,
And the blue riders on their blanketed horses,
Slowly pacing the gutters

                              stiff in the night wind.

SIGILLUM

IF ANY man has despaired, and held his tongue
Over short-circuited life and death, his honor
Prevails in itself, inviolable there.
Hurricane warnings offer a kind of humor.

We who are lapped in the small yellow flames
Of our past days, the sinews of that man,
Acknowledge comets despatched in the galaxy,
A chorus trained more simply than our own.

No season detains our migratory peace,
But it must ever wane, as the boughs of the spirit,
Tired with wind, let fall a trash of leaves;
But it must flow again in the heart's luxuriance,
Not orbital nor elliptical, dearest spring.

QUI CARNEM DECERNIT

DEATH under the fingernails is unreal. The fact
Heaves in the blood, jammed there, cloud as it may.
Squander warmth bitterly, it grows, choking
Caught twigs of thought in massed passion, slowly
Whelms thrust with sluggish weight. Keenly
Clenching the eye push into bone wisp, see
How thick the shadow is, teems, is prodigious,
Stored with time. The antennae of lightning
Search density horribly and go out.

SOLIPSIST

My soiled scholastic body in the pit,
Fixture of mortal apperception.
Sweet light, sweet dream ... The dry skin
Lifted by inquisitors, the skull
Stained in the vats. By this penetration
The essence burns its sphere.

And if my love's two hands are beautiful
And her demeanor modest and wise
And grace going with her to make the heart cry out —
Neither is this a frailty in metaphysic,
For by this penetration is made clear
What light has mastery over vision.

And while the engines live
Within their dizzying motion, no allegories
Tragedies or cartoons esteem them truly
As I, who by this mastery retain
Steel, skull, and space in my domain.

And have no fear.

MIRACLE AT ACAPULCO

THE BABY born, a petal of prophecy
In Mexico, the stone land,
Squirming and speaking:
                    Death
Stands beyond your great eyes,
Moving upon the bronze screen.
Do not sever me, lest the world
Be crushed below light and dark:
But choose among you, speak
In your rushing voices, elect
Fire on the bitten corn, or the mirage
Of earthquake in the gardens . . .

They drew the crucifix with their brown hands
And there in the light under them the child
Withered and spoke no more.

A sign told by the people at their fountains.

IN THIS HOUSE

In this house of the untidy lamp, a
Man is leafing lexicons, his
Limpid fingers in forgotten
Brains. The street mist, ghostwave, laps
His threshold, whereon the traveler stays,
Married thus to a stone
With textual emendations.

Who dreamt he bedded with a whore
's face, body of a child. In a hotel in
Helsingfors. Before the war.

Who will not sleep,
Thinking of the children of women.
Many of them in many houses
Unsleeping.

And of Shuster the rebellious millionaire
Satirized by Persius
Whom many editors are inclined to

Invite to tea . . . From the repose of their souls
O Lord deliver us . . .
So? You are well acquainted.

PERSPECTIVE

I TELL you this present, now on the instant, quick
Dazzled with history our passion lightens.
See, the arteries of the body ravel out
Fiery threads, the fair
And cherished flesh a keen vapor
Of vision blows in the holocaust:
Just as the old poets would say, that time
Eats up sweet love and dainty coupling,
Love consubstantial, the restful world,
Transfigured in this pale blaze expires.

COSMOLOGY

LIFTING yesterday's body in the light:
Wide lonely circles and the head a stone,
A planet picked out in exploded night.
The clouds are clouds of stars, the calmly grown

Flower of time assumes its sudden stem.
In this heavenly surf the world is hung
Without a sound and lustrous like a gem,
The vision that is not inscribed nor sung.

AUBADE

THE GNARLED clouds pacing by the day star
Lift up dawn from gesturing orchestras,
Adagio burning in the piston glow.

The stain spreads over heaven.

A man walks, morose and beautiful
In his own mist, the taste of refuse
Of night like powder fallen in the street.

Earth quickens in the nebula
With jetting stoves, pet-pet of motors,
Heel-beat on grill.

O Lord Apollo
Holy fane and wind vane shining, clear
Glass stunned by the sun —
                              the waves
Doff purest laces, sails, doves on the water.

METAPHYSICIAN

His LOGIC unperturbed, exacting new
Tribute in turbulence, a tithe of motion:

Runners by whose feet daylight is shaken,
Moths, mantles wind-wrought, released sharply
Against throned columns, shafts closing in air —

Attend. Time's clear device in each man's eye
Makes shadows what he sees, and streets shadows
Wherein we move, impelled or quieted;

We have been out to see the latest signs
Unbent from heaven, and these who staring walk
Beside us are not blind, and all who see
Through this low draft of shade will be undone ...

Thus to lie one night with his back broken
And dream at dawn the idol in the stone.

JANUARY NIGHT

                  MOON burnished
Ethereal night, the air burns frailer motion,
Dusting unearthly veils over the steel.
Face the wind and walk your dwindled ghost
Out of a colder distance than at sea
The delicate waves mutter.

                The silk worm spinning
Attenuates its summer's ravishment
For ravished time to follow, and so would he
Who crisps in the combustion of a street lamp.

Mortal tissue, like white mist of the sky
Drifted from the galactic edge, laughter
Solidifies in all-night restaurants, where
At midnight motion stays. O light
Is there a blessing common to our eyes?
O time, unsyllabled thy benediction.

In the ripe air the smoke puts up its tendrils
Wavering to a consummate void. The trays
Slide and are piled. The voices, you and I,
Lead counterpoint to microcosmic clatter
Below our eyes and hands:
Mirror melting in mirror a thousand ways . . .
The dead cannot but taste this honeycomb.
In their pure presences the flowering brow
Of this divinity, as in a crystal,
Flushes forever, as in the rose of time
West of Andromeda the gigantic lens

Strains inward to the heart the clouds of heaven,
Substance of all things loved.

                                Therefore return,
World without end, world without end of splendor,
To climb alone the measurable stairs.

PARK AVENUE

BETWEEN dinner and death the crowds shadow
     the loom of steel.
Engines dwell among the races; the tragic phrase
Falls silent in the tune and tremble of them.
Spun beyond the sign of the Virgin and bloomed
     with light
The globe leans into spring;
The daughter from the dead land returns.
Between the edges of her thighs desire and cruelty
Make their twin temples, whereof the columns sunder
In the reverberations of time past and to come.
A pestilence among us gives us life.
Sparks shot to the cylinders explode softly
Sheathing speed in sleep.

MANUSCRIPT WITH ILLUMINATION

SEVERAL of us are quiet in a ring
Kneeling with taws tight to our dirty thumbs
Or sunlight splitting the serge-shine
Of knickerbockers. Several will be
Braggarts in the shouting yard, or telling
Tremulous others they may see a woman.
Afternoon and dust behind the furnace
Drive the smallest ones to madness. They whack
Lathes in laughter, are afraid. One trussed
Feels his face grow purple, left alone
Cries like a martyr and plots murder.

Among us there will come stately men
Demanding the years of the popes, the seven
Capital sins, or morning in the sacristy.
About their straight cassocks and their pride
Nuns flutter, black and white, the floating doves.
A month's dear guilt is harvest to these men,
Who take our terror, flowers of our terror,
Into God's peace, drowsy with murmured Latin.
There will be several pure before the shutter.

Grace of a happy death.

Several of us are quiet, there is one
Lives with a bitch in Ephesus, another
Dealer in jewels and watches toward the sunrise.
That one, a milksop whiner, is grown ruddy
With iron shots and sunning in the south;

The elevated trembles for his friend
Who counts in a cold room items of love.
Glory in his sweet fold of ancestors
Makes one weep, as anchor chains in mist
Rush from winches for a final landfall.
Others have copious mail, deep marriages.

How earth pulls us and pulls the moon
Our bones know casually. We are diminished
Who grow with treasure of certainty toward
Delicate gestures, smiling in the rooms;
Likewise our desperate shifts for
Appeasement of the beast, the spirit,
Walking in darkness and the check from home,
Waste us wanderers. Several will be
Sheeted in wards, others give autographs,
And one perhaps will live in a cool place,
Devoted to Greek participial loveliness.

Grant them peace.

Sunlight through lightning, or the violins
Falling before the flute. This is the evening
Prophesied by our hearts, and now our love
Builds over summer drouth its structural silence.
There is nothing now but applause of leaves
For the moth's splendor, for the singing
Lute, for crimes ignoble on the stair,
And for our prayers, dubious and tender.

THE WOUND is stiffened in the chest, and the equerries
Shut their blue fists in their trouser pockets.
Smoke falls in the early morning by the door.
A packet of excellent spices is come from India
To be preserved for His Grace's funeral,
The seventh duke, and to his heirs forever,
Recipients of these arms. The lady is twice bereft.
Over the stairs the armored light, drifting
Moves the hours, the absent voices, and the dark
Shepherds, the color of their eyes like leaves.

Yesterday Mr. Hamilton is reported to have spoken
About new hangings for the west hall. His sword.
And mention of an old league broken in the Low
        Countries. Years ago
When the child died the prior rode from the abbey
A wet mare, and in he came, blowing his hands.
Tonight we'll have snow. Do you remember Cockrell?
They were all in there singing by the fire
And the window all of a sudden smashed in, and those
        bastards . . .
That was the autumn. Nothing from the queen,
Whose business is muffled up in Austria
Spain, Flanders, the south sailings and the west.

My friend
Lacing his leather on with surgeon's hands,
Pale as Jesus he was, the groveling toad
Through ice-rime after the lanterns, lurching,

Pikes, mattocks, the whole country crossed with light.
Here are the stones and ossuaries, graves,
Memorials of mice that scratch and perish,
The elegiacs cut with considered pride.
Pain on the right side when you turn, cough badly,
Find no record of service. The old nurse in the park
Visits me sometimes but I'm lonely here.
If you like, the little man who brings wood in the evening,
He would know; he says it was a fine cortège.

EPITHALAMION

LIE DOWN this evening. Firelight, western star
Burn soft within your fêted west, your mother's.
The night of multitudes is still. O grave
Angel of memory, tell our true distress,
Whose love deep generations prison.

A longer wind than on Catullus' eve
Cooled the blinded king. World and world end
Who is this woman now and who is he
Who prays nightlong at her pitied lips?

PETIT JOUR

A COLD light for orisons. Reflect
Upon the diver ascending fathoms five.
Rumple the newest skull and genuflect.
Father, since our scholastic members thrive,
May we compel this world for clasp of thee,
Seeing, as morning flares and night's imagined
Mist dries from the air like memory,
The sun's transparent basin licked by wind.
Therein be instruments fittingly strung
To sound the enviable surf aloud,
While we whose business is not old nor young
Compose in winter light the winter cloud,
Returning when thy creative interval
Has taken down the evening from the wall.

A WREATH FOR THE SEA
1935–1943

haec parva caro patri
virtutis feci memor

COUNSELORS

Whom should I consult? Philosophers
Are happy in their homes and seminars.
See this one with the mischievous bright childlike
Gaze going out through walls and air,
A tangent to the bent rays of the star.
Hear the chalk splutter, hear the groping voice:
Conceive the demiurge in his perpetual
Strife with the chaos of the universe,
That humming equilibrium of creation
Pure and enormous, crossed by the constant
Light of unimaginable combustion:
Teems, how it teems. An elm tree sighs
Beyond the dusty windowledge of June.
As in the mind the notes of a melody
Vibrate when vibration's gone, a series
Generated by a decimal has no end;
Observe it closely, though; it stops when it stops.
The frail spectacles are bedimmed with spring.

But whom should I consult? Well-seasoned men,
Ruddy with business or the salty summer,
Autumnal in their woolens, gaze
Toward the quick plumes above the city.
A frosty morning sun reddens the river.
This one is meditative and well-qualified:
Decently shined, one heavy saddle-dark
Perforated brogan swings from the swivel
Chair arm; leaning back, the head
Well-cropped and grey, the experienced

Eyes quiet, with one highlighted pupil.
A reader of Herodotus in the evening.
The road was in receivership, the mills
Were in receivership, the bondholders
Suitably informed would not dissent
From an able plan of reorganization.
Easy did it.

                And his beautiful daughters
Sink in a circle of white skirts like daisies,
Laughing for the brash photographer.
Years ago they sailed to the North Cape,
Made out that flecked mass in the East
With Mother and the broad-shouldered boy
    from Cook's
On deck in the dim summer on the grey
Sea. Often they saw the fishermen
Off Cherbourg in the awe of morning hitting
The outside spanking seas: red sails in sea-light.
Far away in the nursery a music box
Plucks its icy Bavarian tune for them.

Then whom? A thousand flashes from Long Island
Enter the high room in the office building,
A heliograph of cars turning toward sunset.
Will he decipher them? The journalist
Sweats in his shirtsleeves, mutilates
Cigarettes in a smouldering tray, surveys
Me and the world in a racket of teletypes,
Sick of it and excited, needing a drink.
Positive copy sprouts from the typewriter,
Each paragraph a piston stroke. The sun

48

Glitters on Hackensack, sorrows on the land,
Goes out like a pliant egg sucked down a bottle.
Under the shadowing azure a violet
Dusk consumes the sharp walls of the world.
The melancholy distributor of wit
Snatches at straws amid the alien darkness,
A whirl of dusty danger.

                              For his retreat
The priest lifts up the monstrance, muttering
Abstracted Latin to the tinkle behind him.
Presently they will bawl the Stabat Mater.
And all those years at seminary, reading
St. Basil and Jerome, girding his cassock
For handball in the gritty cement courtyard
Under the swooping smoke of the powerhouse;
And ordination when the folks from Chicago
Wept before the bishop. Mortify
The flesh. Think on thy last end. Pray
The Holy Mother of God in her infinite mercy,
And Him who rests in the dark chapel always,
Where the wick burns in wax, a cuddling flame:
Deduced by Thomas from the tip of heaven.

Or should I tumble to the recumbent
Confessional, and the scientist of distress?
For any child the terror in the night,
The hating eyes by day may be
Death's cunning orchestration: they prepare
The servant's cry at last, absolute and lonely.
See this easy gentleman in tweeds,
Deepchested, a swimmer to the farthest light,

Diagnostician of the subaqueous
Faces of dreams: with patience like a lover
He must all day sustain his authority,
Must not be bored, merciful or amused.

Or the anatomist and healer of bones?
Trepanner, skilled in suturing, the masked
And sterile hero in the cone of light;
There the sweet ether cone must be inhaled
With one, two pulses of the fiery spiral
Singing into timeless speed or quiet:
A mound under a sheet, a square of pale
Mortal flesh incised in a seeping line,
Spreading its lips for pretty butchery.

Blankets, hypodermics and high fever,
Racing delirium in the ward; the tall screen
Efficiently deployed at the bedside;
Intravenous ministrations: charts: starch:
And how is he today. Pretty good, doc.
Or else the fly sits down on the dead face
In the dead sunny room.

                    Shall I have speech
With those undone by the world's great memory?
Men translated by music, treasurers
Of the French phrase, the childhood images,
Unregarded announcers of prophecy;
Staring blind at the stained wall paper
In their nightly rooms; their dreadful hearts
Beating the beds where other hearts have slept

Like birds under the night wind of time.
See this one whom the currents under earth
Intoxicate, and the flosses of the sky:
Weeping, weeping in vanity and grief
He walks toward remote dawn in the empty city,
Facing the cold draft, fish-smell from the river,
Necessitous of love. Masters of intricate
Fancy, libertines of intelligence,
Terrorizers of themselves, laughers in
Language and priests of any mystery —
Not by authority.

What of the revered
Historian, the painstaking public man?
His dusty briefcase worn to a splitting bulge,
The scholar descending from the library
Smiles at the doves, and at the glowing grass.
Letters gone frail and yellow in their strings
Spill fuzz and dust from the stuck folds:
It might be inferred from what the ambassador
Wrote to his daughter in Virginia
That others were privy to the situation.
These judges are gentle and well-cultivated
Honorable stylists, penetrating men,
Mirrors of duplicity and bewilderment,
Mirrors of magnificent deep-rooted structural
Policy and implacable miscarriage.
The documents are all photostated, the files
Arranged. Let humane logic
Guide them in the wilderness of the State.
The pallid husbandman grunts at his fields,

Sells his new lambs in the damp of March,
Thumbs the slick catalogue of the mail order
House for ginghams for the girls of summer;
Chews with the county agent at the gate.
He will be ruddy as the sun goes over,
The clouds go over, the tractor shudders on
Through the high fields. The piling west will grow
Fractious with lightning, the wild branches bend,
Curtains blow out like goodbye handkerchiefs
Hilarious in the gloomy wind. Autumn
Comes with marriages to the aging house,
Winter comes with comforts and old death.
Still the farmer's dull hand holds the seed;
The low star glimmers on the dewy sill.

HORAE

I. IT PALES. As if a look,
Invisible, came in the east.
In some far vale a rooster
Expels his cry of life.

Now dark but not formless
On the grey meads the trees
Lean and are looming soft.

In those towers of night
Ruffling things awake
Their declaration and chuckle.

Starpoint fades from the dew.

To every mile that sleeps
The cock's barbaric cry
And the wind comes cool.

Shiver of day break.

II. Now air, gentle pillager
In the citadels of summer,
Lifts a leaf here and there.
Sun holds the cornfield still
In his dream of the real.

From a wavering of bees
One droning steers away,
Elated in his golden car.
A cow stumbles and streams,
Reaching the meadow.

Tiny brutality in the grass
Manipulates the foe
Sawing and champing. Oh, soundless.

What burning contemplation
Rests in these distances?
What is seen by the leaves
Mirrored as in fair water
Millionfold? — as the eye of man
Finds itself in myriads.

III. The limber shadow is longer.
Air moves now breathing
In the plumes of corn.

Gnats on their elastics
Are busy with evening.
Heavy with night, the owl
Floats through the forest.

Shadow takes all the grass.

Beyond indigo mountains
Golden sheaves are fastened
Lightly on the infinite
West. What joy or feast
Has these for ornament?
What reclining host?

They sink away in peace.

CELESTINE

I. The mother fragrant in her dust and grace,
With leaflike generations burning,
Was not that mother but a grander kind;
And they would know her bloomed, luxurious turning
Through the deep ballroom's flawless glass:
A queen of iron port and accurate pace,
Who led, as with gigantic mind,
The partner facing her through night and noon,
Enthralled by power of pure mass,
Her sister, the naked moon.

II. Whose intensive rondure filling the spring
Night with radiance, or low
Each evening after reaping in the north,
Beautiful vessel of the afterglow,
All being quiet and all free,
In sexual love or restful lingering
At her most certain coming forth,
They smiled to name their goddess, like a swan
That in the nightstream silently
Took her perfection on.

III. The silver flame in the washed western air
Clear, shivering and bright,
Love's bridal star, would not come punctual there
For she was of those lamps that moved alone;
And they were sunlit worlds, to man's frail eyes
Reflecting the cyclonic furnace light
That still so distant shone,

The golden focus of their paradise;
Round whom in harmony of measured haste
They tended, and receded slower-paced.

IV. The spheres' artificer dreamed out his hour,
Yet this was not revealed;
Not to the watcher in the starlit tower,
Blinded with noting transits on his rim —
Though he had seen the wandering planet run,
Stay and return upon the heavenly field,
And had recorded him;
But to that intellect which is itself a sun,
Of pitiful light the source, and source of flame:
In Prague to Kepler the great vision came.

V. And radiance ruled the firmament.
The massy centers were outflown.
Out of that void of ghostly gossamers
The stars that shone upon the innocent
For chemic flares were known.
The icy constellations came and went,
But fastened upon alpha's height
The driving-clock astronomers
Brought nearer from the sprinkled vast
The blazing body of the night;
And still the whorls beyond, and still and still
In points of cepheids and laggard light
Beyond mindsight or lens, the last
Marches of that giant Past
Faint upon the intense invisible.

ANIMULA

I. THE WORLD of substance where I chuckled first,
And goggled, balancing my enormous noddle —
To remember remembering and not remember —
Dipped into such backward shade, that time,
As snapshots fade in; yet it is dearly dim.
Little and big: littleness belonged to me,
And bigness from the bear-dark of the staircase
Called me in a new mystery of nightfall.
I love my father forever
Whose hail came through the shuddering angelus;
Of her death nothing rises from the dark.

II. Bright splinters, tangible, run from a winter time.
The rounded snow, a granular cold crust,
Clung at a window, sapped by the bare day light.
A leaden soldier seemed perpetual.
A pretty woman toweling my cheek
Would lay it close to hers: drier and warmer.
The glossy rubbers snapping, and the toiling
Fitting of toes through gaiters, pushing thumbs
Into white fuzzy mittens: then the cold,
The nose-anesthetizing cold, the yard
A black-eyed snowman's sordid and fair kingdom.
A world of twigs and snow-birds and low sun,
Blue shadow and black wires overhead,
A wagon crunching, a train bell's clang clang
Over so many fences, and icy gardens
Where iron nymphs froze at the fountain bowls.

No breath was in that air invisible
But winter's, that made the dead leaf scrape.

III. The rarity, the silver of that season
I would lay hold of, were I only spirit;
The great nights, too, and their cracking stillness
Powdered with stars of snow, and cold, cold;
Jack Frost at work; his handiwork of fern.

The wondering and minuscular fore-finger
Traced that embossing by the magic world.
Powdery sugar in a cut glass and silver
Shaker might be held, massy and lovely,
With such cool facets, like so much of winter;
The dressmaker pouting pins, technic of scissors
Whisking their shearing way beneath her thumb's
Cocked and incredible ability,
The lightning needle of the sewing machine —
All at eye-level, moved in the vast interior:
Lightless halls, cold air of attic stairs,
The under side of elbows and of chins,
And a trousered or an aproned leg to lean on.
Along the floor under the bed was cold.

LOOK. Look. On the outer glass
Raindrop gathers and glides, crooked.
Tin spout gushes a whitish water.
Street dances: ranks of rain.
Treetrunk inky, and twigs. Darkening
Past twelve. April. The bronze clock
Ticks. Dry carpet prickles knees.

Turn on the lights. Electric yellow
Light on the greylight. Aching now,
Elbows mashed on the tintsheet. Slim Jim
Eluding less lank cops: gone
Up the rainspout. Terrible kids,
Katzenjammers. Come now, child,
Dinner. Do you hear? I'm coming.

Cheek sore, crushed on hand.
Your hands washed?
                         Larger, denser,
Commanders, jokers, dark-heavy dressers,
Odorous, either scent or cigars.
The men are mountains: they play mountains,
Avalanches drop from their shoulders,
Rumbling down the vest valleys
Grainy and hot. Their huge napkins
Spread like snow on laps and knees.
So stupid. Do not let them know.

EVENING PRAYER

WITH these O God these
sins of the light prayers were
reserved for sleep

forehead of childhood
and the dark take care
take all your sight inside

night night the blanket grave
the smell of blanket breathing
sleep dimness the beasts

come soft shaken and the eyes
across nothing like air
O God my words in darkness

to be warm to be brave to
go packed in armor rising
sometimes in air

stoneweary knees
and to you father
sleep sleep sleep sleep

grass and lilac and
through my most grievous fault
the beast is unappeased

the agony in the garden
now I unclasp my hands
into thy hands my spirit

A SQUARE of sucking brilliance in the dark.
Over it in the depth and distance a rider
Leaving a comet's furrow of dust. Blink:
Down the gigantic mountain the booted daredevil
Twists the piebald, making play with his bridle:
The savior of the overland stage.
                                        Why, ma'am,
That wasn't no ride atall. Well, Miss Ginger,
Guess I aint ever seen a gal so purty.

Gingham rounded, the breathing bosom shows
Under tight hands. Nearer, the forms distend.
Smooth and vast, her yielding visage slopes
Backward and opens: cheekbones and mouth-molding,
Temples and wide eyes: the beseeching gaze
Casts from eye to eye of the dauntless hero:
Is it love? Oh, is it love, Dusty?
Fuses at last in obliterating clinch.

Matinee: a nickel. The outside, acid air
Alien and cold. Twilight and lights downtown.
Pedestrians huddled in their hurrying strangeness.
Phantasms draining from the ominous world,
Sang froid from the doped urchin. The way home.

PATRUUS

OUTSTARING Furies in simple night; bastard of Night!

Will not be coward with these sheep, will take as he please
Whiskey or any whore's groove, grossly virginal, strike
And vomit out this anger, break the false world down,
Fight bloody in an alley with brakeman or boxer —
                                                He who would wish
Evening to be kittenwarm, fresh fires, and at ease
In a deep chair-pit crackling his new-cut creamy pages —
His grin a narrowing birdflight over sunset face —
To revel nodding with Carlyle or Dr. Syntax or
      George Borrow.

With what remorse of rivers his military laughter comes
From the jetting caverns of his heart to affright the child,
Whose toes in-pointing and beseeching never move.

Now lightning fix forever the pistol rims of his eyes,
The raging nightmare of his wit! He is not one
Apparition to himself; his courage like a great cat
Plies before innocence, and he, too, innocent,
Gazes aside down spinning time to a helpless country,
Quiet and far away. Dust rising from thin wagons
In an autumn square. Grave trees, all gaunt and
      garlanded.

ADULESCENTIA

I WOULD articulate
By incantation, more than a tale could say
Of that clear lake and dazzlement of youth,
Mercury wherein the nerved body's lightness
Floated trembling or dazed;
Shame's burning kingdom, vanity's new world.

Miraculously, through prayer to Saint Anthony,
The lost tennis ball was found in the alders:
That dun, worn, airy to-be-bounced
Treasurable and humble dweller in closets.

Charms lived in patterns: on the red-brick chevrons
Propriety went splayfooted or pigeontoed.
Old Valentines were aching amulets.
Tenting, the air rifle by the bed was trusty.

Yet where the leaf quaked or the acorn snapped,
Something held its breath in the tight dark.
God, let there be some midnight walker,
Heavy-heeled and solid; let me turn over.

Let the bright business day come soon, for kitchen's
Or gasoline's keen odor.
                              By the machinist
In his dark shop, his dim lamp taped and caged,
A savory leather belt ran on and on, round
The clotted motor's flywheel. Vises, greasy
Roundheaded hammers, the black hands of skill,
And the rough shed suffered the spectator.

As likewise the slow, aproned carpenter
Fitting his fragrant, never-niggled
Solids of purity with decisive art.

Yet all in awkwardness the day dream
Elevated its presently clear forms:
Prowess and grace of the invulnerable
Courteous horseman, the silk-shirted fencer
Far from the salle-d'armes, scraping and ringing;
The aviator fixing his tracer stream
On some nefarious Fokker; clean-cut Stover
Indomitable in the roaring bowl.

The lamb of God that washed away the world's
Sins proffered for combat and emulation
His terrible prudery.
Helplessly implicated and endowed
With the invaluable carnal slug:
Absolve me, O God, from the drugged, furtive
Minute at the magazine counter. Absolve
The clenched panic of the animal swelling,
The intolerable devouring of the image.

How, by what structure, by what music,
In what weaving way could I make visible
The incongruity and glory?

Through listlessness and fatigued silence of summer
Henry Esmond bent amid English autumn
Over the grave of his dear lady.
Cheerful, the swordsman penned his fresh paragraph;
The fond prince dangled after the daring belle.

Beatrix, be my ribboned and sweet love!
All dust, all generations.

And shadowy history stormed upon the mind
When age, most beautiful in taffeta,
Roamed quietly among the mounds and urns.
That turf, those lonely sprays,
Her gentlemanly boys commemorated.

Of actual ignobility too proud
To admit brotherhood, and sickened
By the known world's casually sweating
Stupor, savagery and injustice,
Shamefast and haughty, that time passed.

COBB WOULD HAVE CAUGHT IT

In SUNBURNT parks where Sundays lie,
Or the wide wastes beyond the cities,
Teams in grey deploy through sunlight.

Talk it up, boys, a little practice.

Coming in stubby and fast, the baseman
Gathers a grounder in fat green grass,
Picks it stinging and clipped as wit
Into the leather: a swinging step
Wings it deadeye down to first.
Smack. Oh, attaboy, attyoldboy.

Catcher reverses his cap, pulls down
Sweaty casque, and squats in the dust:
Pitcher rubs new ball on his pants,
Chewing, puts a jet behind him;
Nods past batter, taking his time.
Batter settles, tugs at his cap:
A spinning ball: step and swing to it,
Caught like a cheek before it ducks
By shivery hickory: socko, baby:
Cleats dig into dust. Outfielder,
On his way, looking over shoulder,
Makes it a triple. A long peg home.

Innings and afternoons. Fly lost in sunset.
Throwing arm gone bad. There's your old
    ball game.
Cool reek of the field. Reek of companions.

66

SEA PIECES

I. SEPTEMBER six o'clock:
The young tinted faces
Pale in the harbor.

The sail falls shaking;
The water smiles from the prow.

Low sun, a cooler light
Exhaled; low evening stains
Waterblue under beeches.

The longlegged children
Are furling their sails
In the air like clear water,

The water like air, like mist.

II. Cool cheek to cheek
And long gaze of children:

Mark how the gull's intent
Wings half-golden
Tremble in sea-flaw.

Hand in hand, warm thought
To lie together, as light
Leaves the dark land of ocean:

Pallor above purple
Slow horizons fuming

Evening, star of the sea.

ECCE ABSTULISTIS HOMINEM
DE HAC VITA

Low in the barren winter
The dark rain stopped at dawn,

And the muddy cans of iron
Leaned in the ashen lanes.

The sparrows were all silent.
The night lamps were grey.

I turned to the faces.
I turned from the faces.

No. No.

And the alleys offered their sorrow,
The gutters their cold tears.

The dandelions were old,
The acorn pipe was broken.

The firecrackers were spent
And the Roman candles empty.

The Christmas seals were torn
And the tissue torn forever.

I looked into forever.
I saw the black forever.

No. No.

And the alleys offered their sorrow,
The gutters their cold tears.

The algebra and the graphs
And the zodiac were weeping.

The sundial in the fog
Endured it, weeping.

In the frayed dictionary
There were no synonyms.

I opened the door of death.
I could not see my death.

No. No.

And the alleys offered their sorrow,
The gutters their cold tears.

The Jack-knife and the Daisy
Rifle, stiff with rust,

And the old tasseled saber,
The shadowy water jug,

The razor and the mirror —
Hell stared there forever.

I went to the window.
I went to the door.

No. No.

And the alleys offered their sorrow,
The gutters their cold tears.

ET QUIDQUID ASPICIEBAM
MORS ERAT

"IN THIS and whatever days to come
The transparent world and its motions
Compose a sheer void. How could
That be removed upon which every
Animate joy was founded? What
Thrives now but the vile face of nature
Made up by the sun to idiot glory?
Let it sway and blow its intrinsic
Monotony of vapors, seasons,
Tumblebugs and blind men; let me
Weep and curse those begetting fools,
And honorably weep my life long.

"You would not cover me over
With the dropping indecent clods,
You sanctimonious bastards: take
Such of my hatred as is left
When I have cursed the aspergent
Water shaker with his stole, his
Sotto voce Latin sing song;
You craving, self-important ghouls,
Let me alone, or I will show you
The savage green sprouting
Through the obscene holes of your eyes.

"Gone out of the air, not gone
Out of my nightly vision, yet
With desperate years to be corrupted
There too, wasted, thinned

To the damned ghost of your convention —
You win in the end — he who was
So distinguished for patience,
For suffering, for valor,
Of such sensible pale fingers,
A humorous, wise man.

"Hereby I curse this hard city
And its whoring, golfing, political
Poker-playing men, all those
Who were schoolfellows or friends
In the old time, and never,
Though good churchgoers, visited him.
And I engrave here my small blessing
On that large silent decent one
Who thought it friendliness to do so;
Him and few others would I spare,
But let the rest go rot in a worse
Hell than even their own world is.
Yet their unawareness is his grace,
If grace be in this charnel progress:
His ten-year sickroom I say
Shames with life their death forever,
And all is death elsewhere."

SOULS LAKE

The evergreen shadow and the pale magnolia
Stripping slowly to the air of May
Stood still in the night of the honey trees.
At rest above a star pool with my friends,
Beside that grove most fit for elegies,
I made my phrase to out-enchant the night.

The epithalamion, the hush were due,
For I had fasted and gone blind to see
What night might be beyond our passages;
Those stars so chevalier in fearful heaven
Could not but lay their steel aside and come
With a grave glitter into my low room.

Vague though the population of the earth
Lay stretched and dry below the cypresses,
It was not round-about but in my night,
Bone of my bone, as an old man would say;
And all its stone weighed my mortality;
The pool would be my body and my eyes,

The air my garment and material
Whereof that wateriness and mirror lived —
The colorable, meek and limpid world.
Though I had sworn my element alien
To the pure mind of night, the cold princes,
Behold them there, and both worlds were the same.

The heart's planet seemed not so lonely then,
Seeing what kin it found in that reclining.

And ah, though sweet the catch of your chorales,
I heard no singing there among my friends;
But still were the great waves, the lions shining,
And infinite still the discourse of the night.

MUTATIONS

I. THE ABSOLUTE dark: and if you say, A cloud —
I say: I've spun abroad, often, with them.
What though I cherish her, tanned thigh,
Stovelight of pleasure: I who saw the sea
With more than wind making it seethe, the waves
Fawning toward her beauty? I who smiled
At festal summer, jested, remarked the morning,
Smile now for nothing, like a jaded Punch:
Nerve-net, bone-dangle, visceral-slick piping
My too-late company, my table friends.

II. Child cries at nightfall, man when beyond
      himself
Cast by his love, which is his loneliness.
Nightly he watches the fan-silken beams
Mix their bright haze and waver over hills,
And lies with her against his darkness then.

ANTIQUIORA

THAT was. All that was.
The mounds of the cities.
The dust of the tombs. All that.

Slow: distant: shimmer of flocks
On gentle mountain: softer than forest:
Pouring from the vale like cloud:

Ranging: mild: herds of heaven:
Sunherds: driven by rainy hounds:
East breath from high land: south
Fire wind of the waste: tawny:

Eyelash shadows in the vast:
Herdsmen, focus of sun-circle:
Center of nearer night's rim:
Godstar bright in the blue dusking:

The pot ceiling of flame's house:
Warm to hands: remember rivers
Where the yellow god rises:
Nightmist rises out of earth:

Mother of men: mother of rivers:

Bowstring thrums in the dry autumn:
Deer bleeds, swung by the hocks:
Fires, feasting and flute playing:
Pelt soft for the child's tumble:

Night: enter the still woman:
Rest in cavern under the boughs
Silent: hear in the late dark
Sigh and siffle: the snow wind:

Come down then to the dark ocean:

HELLAS

THE YOUNG blind fellow saw the wind
Ruffle that pacing loveliness,
The sun of Asia on her shoulder.

Unsmiling in his great humored song
He glanced toward her: western her love
Over the long years' lapping water
Lay in her dear land, Lacedaemon.

At the west gate the gaffers wheezed
Their cricket whispers after her.

A SUMPTUOUS moss hoods the skull
Of the old soldier; the rich seasons
Inter him with their gradual commentary, —
Like the fair Latin of the gownsman,
An old idiom unsavored nowadays
But here and there by some dreading poet.

The actual oblivious world being
Sum of his seeking and his fear:
That west where the flashing ocean fell
Toward Orient spiceries of fable,
Those passages amid islands and gulls
Strange to the cumbered arquebusier,
Burn yet with his beautiful valor.

The innocent who never saw his king
But forced for him the virgin lakeland,
Entered the black flood, and toiled
With a saint's cry in a sea of archers.
The crossed sticks of his reverence
Kept him a child through wounds and sins.

Whom fallen on his cut knees and hands
A feathery patriciate so justly
Bore to an agony we cannot know;
That ritual too the study of abstracted
Time puts by, forming fresh elegies
In the cold singing dream of the spirit.

The spires of Puebla and Compostela
Converse of him in their slow canticles
Of Vesper, midnight and morning-shine;
The tone of their struck aerial burden

Alto to the drone of murderous men;
As likewise the palm rustles of Cadiz
And Guatemala have imperceptible
Sea-speech of one another; the wine
Smell in the streets and the rainwater
Under the sun in the stone cisterns
Insist on commemorating him;
And over the acerbic trolley sparks
His fallen rampart is golden.

ATLANTIC SONG

HEAVING about Cornwall stone, gold
Combers unfurled from western tempest
Lace the glistering ocean's heel:
Granite, fanned to its speechless rim,
Ringing Merlin's world in azure.
Here through the world's dread shadow
Horsemen in iron bosses rode
Through nightmeadow and savage wood
To the charred tower, the stone pool,
Glared upon by a hairy star.

Whose home was in the wave of the west.

My home is on the smoking billow
With stormboys of the western world,
And their derisive pikemen roaring
Under the swaying and faraway
Foaming ocean of Land's End.
O milkwhite maid the sea rolls over,
Their bitter shrouds unfurled by tempest
Tumble ashore your virgin laces!

See, the old world, its scudding emblems
Fixed on the pale shield of heaven,
Roll in our salty western light —
Bright scuppers and shot buckets, wind
Northeasterly, fair, following
On the long, clear capes of summer
To Caroline and Virginia's shore.
O created world, O maiden world,

See the cold heaven of white cloud
Break out the Admiral's evening star!

Our home is in the wave of the west.

DIRECTIVE

SCAN the four quarters or the more minute
Divisions of the stars upon the compass:
The motion of the ranges is against us.

To cross that pass of stone before snowfall
We need a lighter pack on the pack horses.

Keep powder, ball, and venison strips;
Cache the rest; look out for savages;
Note any signal smoke or trace of ponies.

The main party must be at the sweet water.

MEMENTOES

I. THE INLAND cities on the rivers
Stream into the clear morning.
Rust and slag, junk in the marshes,
Where the wind shivers the tall weeds.
From the gliding Pullman see
Steamy light on the weather vanes,
Golden crosses on distant steeples
Risen above the smoke and dew.
A child in a dirty shift watches
From a tumbledown garden or threadbare
Screen door; wide-eyed pickaninnies
Curl their toes in the sweet air.
Slower with swaying jerks and turning
A long curve between factory windows,
Blackened fences, cindery yards,
Enter the early hustle of men:
The grey drayhorses smiting, backing,
On Market Street; mustachioed
Entrepreneurs with golden fobs
Brisk on the cobbles; rumble and yell.

The lumber schooners pass on the lake
And the slow barges from the north
Pass in the offshore bite of whitecaps:
Superior, Erie, Michigan,
Loaded with ore from the wilderness
For the furnaces of Pennsylvania,
Loaded with grain from the cool prairies,
Passing the evergreen shores and the beaches.

The wind out of the south blows over
Brownstone mansions in the sunlight,
A browner haze, bringing the odor
Of blood and offal. The long and short-horns
Crowd from the West, from the lone corrals
Of Kansas, Texas, high Wyoming.
There the sun makes the land shimmer,
Tawny and pale, the vast rangeland;
There the smoke from a locomotive
Worms up slowly all morning long.

Trainmen and rangeriders: remember
The water tanks, the peeling clapboards
The silent noon of desert towns;
Remember the hot nights and whiskey
And silver dollars on the tables;
Remember the women and the badman
Out of the badlands, wiping his mouth;
Goodbye, you fast thumbs on the sixgun,
Knee-ers and rabbit-punchers, dusty
Bastards in from the plains with pay;
Goodbye Belle and Jenny and Mister
LaPorte from St. Louis with yellow vests;
Goodbye to buckboards and Winchesters,
To the hobbled ponies, the trading post.
Cody, pray for us; Wister, bless us;
So long, strangers, so long.

II. Patent leathers and white kid gloves;
Lovely, humiliated or gay,
Arrogant or dreaming with the dance,

They move in grace between the mirrors,
In candle light. The cool odor,
"Cologne," breathes above "bodices,"
And the ever-so-silken, continual
Draping, re-draping of skirts. Hushabye.
Smiles of trust or invitation
Whirl away on lustrous lapels
Laughing under the fiddles. Comely
Shoulders, powdery backs, warm
Flanks under ruffles, smooth elbows,
All are turning in the courteous
Viennese music, end of the century.
Newport, Narragansett, Richmond,
Boston, New York and Baltimore,
Far into morning. Shearing the snow,
The cutters at a good clip jingle
Uphill running into starlight,
Bundled and singing. Stilly night.

Goodbye to all your tears, sweethearts,
And your stern gentlemen at home;
Goodbye to the shy lieutenant, the gigglers,
The convents and the musical studies,
The crushes and the exclamations;
Goodbye to the box at the theater
And the slow fanning in the gaslight;
To summers at Sheepshead Bay, to muslins,
To bare forearms and serenaders,
Ribbons and billets-doux, goodbye.

Milly and Daisy and Henrietta

And Isabel, beauties, pray for us
In your fresh heaven, on those lawns
By Thames under the copper beeches,
Behind the iron gates in ducal
Shadow: ambassadors! At Venice
Where the old and weary and splendid
Spiders of the world devoured you,
Who were not ever in anything
Quite so correct as they. Sisters,
Mothers later corrupted, maidens
Living like men into bewilderment
With a stiff upper lip: you masks
At operas and marriages,
Matriarchs with knobby canes,
Goodbye, goodbye gentlewomen.

STROPHE AND ANTISTROPHE

I. OF HER cold and imperial image
Of her disinterested and fine bearing
Of her swiftness and merit

In winter when Andromeda, sparkling,
Lay on the grey Eastern wave
In summer when Arcturus, golden star
Rose on the lake of shadow

Bare to the snowflake or the sharp leaf
    whirling
His head sang bitterly,
Wandering in unseen evening.

Him I found brother and master,
Who to this artifice and hard chorale
Gave elegance out of love.

Return, return, great fictive lady!

In him the craven, common lie
Broke, and the sadly studying fool,
Mocked by his angry angel.

Return, return, great lady!

By his caught breath and wit were made
Those lettered verses, lambent with memory,
In modes more subtle than dark nightingales
Honey the savage stillness with.

The lady will return.

II. In midland and on hissing water
In black cities and sites of terror
In revels and prisons

Wherever time, most irreproachable
Would take my thick loneliness
Wherever quailing and desire, that surf
Bore my stopped heart fighting

Nerved as an athlete or equestrian,
His brilliance in my dusk
Played a resilient lightning.

Brother and mirror he found me,
Who from his book and from his pride
        of tears
Moved deep into evening.

Return, return, great blessed music!

In me the fat, eternal soul
Winced, and the bones too dull with ruin
Woke to the Latin splendor.

Return, return, great music!

By his art, labored out of love,
Learning and rage, practiced in poverty,
Let me now praise his lady and his song,
Fantast and noble, let me praise him.

The music will return.

WINDSHIELD

A WET day on the road: the slim blades cutting
Fans of transparency among water jewels;
Distension and rip of high-speed passers-by,
Deaf to the lowly gatherings of the field;
Corn tassels tossed and oak leaves flowing in
    darkening
Grey rain and western wind.

                      Unplug the lighter
And frown cross-eyed upon that fiery circlet;
There is always something wanting about our hands,
On just-soft cushions lolling or lightly at work
With the slender wheel; and there is something
Perpetually unsaid in what we say —
Our silken exhalations of being friends.
A failure of no consequence?

                          I've dreamed
Of armless men in carnivals, legless men
Knuckling like apes on smoky avenues,
A world's whole host of savage crippled men
Silent but for the single cry: "Somewhere!"

On each long curve the highway balances
Against our speed with tight terrestrial power,
Conducting to no other place but here;
Here always, the wide alien light of home,
The ever-present wildness of the air —
The nightly dread, say, in cold parishes
Of some tall silvery and unsmiling Father —
A child's wish to do something simply superb.

BEAUTYREST

A TRAINBELL in the windiness, and leaves
Batting the screen of a strange summer morning
Make the house laugh; the little lakes crinkle
Pressed by the breeze that brooms the highway clean.

The midnight traveler was the most distinct,
Whom clouds of maples and late rising stars
Guided, huge baby, to his rickety home.
His motor sighed, shut off under the window,
And then his footstep, creaking, and his groan
Made a disclosure I cannot remember.

It might have been a void, a wandering name,
A tanner, skinner, hooper, waggoner,
Jack of all trades — jackboot, jackknife or jack —
Or bloodshot son of grand O'Rahilly;
Sodbuster's it might be, or sledgeman's son
That from the Adriatic's golden breast
Climbed the black hull in hunger; voyageur,
Porteur, or habitant; or mountain man
His ancient father was, who poled the rivers,
Trapped the fox, and saw the dusk of bison
Grazing on plains of light, or the cold pine
Pillar in the aurora's winter stream.

The late cars on the road and crossing whistles,
Both near and far, were that man's requiem.
At his bedside and feet the starlit rails
And wires wet with dew sang of his cities,

Before dim earth asleep had cabined him,
And cabined him in me.
                          Gone on the grey
Dawngloaming road against the smoking East,
To drowse with sun-up in some distant town —
Not a soul here heard the man so early.

PLAUSIBILITIES

I. FOR THE free cell, the procreator,
Body is sac and ejaculator;
Nothing stays but immortal hunger,

Quest and nerves inseparable.
Testament: on the scholar's wall
The blood-blackened gloves of the boxer.

II. Yet here the warm-hearted master still
        rejoices.
The choir with careful love that never harms
Sing out like angels on his heavenly tune.

Who would not weep at their clear falling
        voices?
The sea whose head is hidden in her arms,
The fair planets shining beyond the moon.

I. I CAME then to the city of my brethren.
Not Carthage, not Alexandria, not London.

The wide blue river cutting through the stone
Arrowy and cool lay down beside her,
And the hazy and shining sea lay in the offing.

Ferries, pouring the foam before them, sliding
Into her groaning timbers, rang and rang;
And the chains tumbled taut in the winches.

Upstream the matted tugs in the heavy water,
Their soiling smoke unwrapped by the salt wind,
Footed with snowy trampling and snowy sound.

On tethers, pointing the way of the tide,
The crusted freighters swung with their sides
    gushing.

On evening's ship pointing northward,
A golden sailor at sunset stood at the bow,
As aloft in the strands a tramcar with tiny
    clanging
Slowly soared over, far upward and humming
    still.

II. Not Athens, Alexandria, Vienna or London.

And evening vast and clean above the city
Washed the high storeys with sea-light, with
    a silken
Sky-tint on the planes and the embrasures:

The clump of crags and glitter sinking eastward
With the slow world, the shadow-lipping shores,
Pale after-conflagration of the air.

On terraces, by windows of tiredness,
The eyes dropped from that glow to the dusk
    atremble,
Alive with its moving atomic monotone:

There the hot taxis at the pounding corner
Fitted their glossy flanks and shifted, waiting,
And the girls went by with wavering tall
    walking,
Their combed heads nodding in the evening:

The hour of shops closing, the cocktail hour,
Lighting desire and cigarettes and lighting
The strange lamps on the streaming avenue.

THE IMPRISONED

I. THE NEWSVENDOR with his hut and crutch
And black palm polished by pennies
Chinked me swiftly my worn-out silver;
Then I went underground.

                           Many went down there,
Down blowing passages and dimness where
Rocketing cars were sucked out of sound in the
      tunnel.

A train came and expired, opening slots to us
All alacritous moving in voiceless numbers,
Haunch to haunch, elbow to hard elbow.

One would sleep, gaping and sagged in a corner,
One might wish for a seat by the girl yonder;
Each a-sway with his useless heavy headpiece.

II. Tenements: "islands" in the ancient city.
Neither under the old law nor the new
Could any insulation make them gentle.

Here I retired, here I did lay me down —

Beyond the washing lines reeled in at evening,
Beyond the roofpots and the lightless skylights,
The elevated grated round a curve
To pick up pitch diminishing toward silence —
And took my ease amid that hardihood:
The virago at her sill obscenely screeching
Or the lutanist plucking away at " My Lady
      Greensleeves."

III. The down beat, off beat, beat.
A hopped up drummer's perfect
Tocking periodicity and abandon.

Cush a cush cush a cush. Whang.
Diddle di daddle di yup yup
Whisper to me daddy. On the
Down, the down beat, beat.

The spot's on blondie, see her croon,
See that remarkable subtle pelvic
Universal joint softly rolling.
Honey take it sweet and slow,
Honey, take your time.
Roll those eyes and send, baby, send.

And swing it, O cats
Express your joys and savoir faire
You hot lick connoisseurs: shake
A laig like New Orleans. Or

Rumba. O you Arthur Murray, O you Murray
        boys
With your snappy steward jackets keeping young,
Steer and sway, you accomplished dancers.
Won't you come over to my table.
Meet Rosemary. This is Rosemary.

IV. The manhole disks were prone shields of
        morning
Where the sun greeted the avenue.

O lumbering conveyances! O yellow
Gliding of cabs, thousand-footed dimpling
      stir!
The fresh net placed on the fair hair!

The steel shutters removed at Tiffany's
And the doorman pulling his beige gloves on;

The elevator boy holding down his yawn
And the cool engineer with his briefcase;

The sun striking over the void city room
And the first hasteners through the concourse;

The riveter walking out on the flaking plank
And the welder donning his goggles;

The steel drawer sliding from the office file
And the receptionist fixing her lipline;

The towsled showgirl a-drool on the pillow
And the schoolyard filling with cries;

The roominghouse suicide at peace by the
      gasjet
And the nun smiling across the ward —

Against the shine of windows, visual
Madness of intersecting multitudes,
Their speech torn to bits in the torrent.

PERFORMERS

I. THE CONJURER'S clever, disavowing hand
Summons from the air an ace of diamonds.
But do not be delighted yet. He pummels
One handkerchief to a combustive morsel
And drapes the stage with banners. But
Do not be delighted yet. Unpent
From feathery nowhere to the dazzled pit,
The doves will clap and close their snowy
    wings!

But do not be delighted yet.

This pirouetting, gesturing savoir
Needs none of your contemptible applause.

II. Here is a window space upon the action,
Unrestful sill and frame: the timber stuck,
Jamming or banging. A proscenium
That opens on the theater from the rear;
The apron, likewise, of a darker stage.

No need to cast your eyes back hither.
Here's a dull player, here's a ranter,
Muffing his lines and propping up a wing.
More than a little odd, this solitary:
See his wild, sweating glances at your party;
Observe his gnarled resentment of décor.

I. To PLACE the precisely slippered toes
With meditation on each stair;
To hold his lurking counterpose
Of anger, smiling to play fair;

To balance with his glittering sea-
Eyes the fragility of bone,
Slender and gaunt as a winter tree —
Studied all grace, and so his own.

To be cat-eyed, slit-eyed, to catch
Astringent nets of namby creatures,
That with articulate despatch
He skewered with their pamby teachers;

To note in the cold Boston bay
The flouncing light on the clean arches;
To know with exact hate the way
A faking builder stuffs and starches;

To stand amid his Where and Whence
With verse in never-ending bout,
To figure some unworldly sense
And keep the melodic nonsense out;

To write a sterner myth than Tate's
Or that of Cummings or of Crane —
Owned and disowned the Concord gates
And Cousin Brooks's sweet terrain.

But saw the heads of death that rode
Within each scoundrel's limousine,
Grinning at hunger on the road
To incorporate the class machine;

And saw the tower of the poor,
Lonely, ignoble, noisy, blind,
With that great Cross upon the Tower.
Fantasy drove him out of mind.

Yet upward in LaFarge's flame
His savior twisted, and does still;
The true line comes as once it came
To masculine Homer's steady will;

Control and charity of the just,
And their wild laughter flung at night,
Commemorate his death, his dust,
His gaiety. John Wheelwright.

II. Morphine more fines they cried within
And just to be precisely more
Redactuate of tit and tin
Convexed a junior editor

To keep the Pentateuch unpent
Or pig it on the whizzy door
His tag was up, his kilter sent
To be a junior editor

Wherries of unwhiggish light
Seasang from the fusty hoar

But Lubgub tub his rubbers tight
And was a junior editor

Figgy and transleafy ching
O summer sobwith freckle o'er
Erotic him; but Lubgubbing
Was still a junior editor

III. Who doubts the fitting key
Who serves another's eye
Whose hand is not his own
Who never thought he won

Who watches the leaf turn
When the rose child is born
Who hears the mouth of death
Repeat a dry myth

The brutal present and the soft past
His constants are; all else is variable;
Through waking weather and the climates of
        dream
That mathematic shapes his character;

As one love-lost, bemused by memory,
He smiles, moves sunny hands, goes out
To April's shadowing air or to machine guns
Punching in dust their rows of periods.

TESTAMENTARY

I. QUIETLY let me put aside the imagist's
Self-satisfaction, the duelist's pride.
All turns of grace are lost. Here is a temple
Whose acrid and charged altars merely
Smoke and abide, ungarlanded, turbines
Hid in a swarming of oblivion.
Trash blows in this congress. One by one
Our scribbled days are torn away; the smiling
In our trick eyes, incredible as tears,
Fades from the corners or the doors quickly.

And love, upon this racket crucified,
Asks of the old, the architectural powers,
To what end they elect such industry;
And the insufferable statistician
Replies: riches.

II. Madmen smooth as ice, sagacious men,
Succeeders and sycophantic men, Petronians,
Flash-bulb boy friends, storkclub habitués,
Iniquitous ascetic men, good fellows,
Levantine family men, Americans,
White men and fashionable wedding men,
Peter Stuyvesant men of mellowness,
Long Island men with lawns, Republicans, —
Ancestral masks in our perpetual
Obsequies, attended as a circus —
In your advertisements the world
Shows forth those portents the diviners read

In other times from birds — the dip of finches,
Possibly, or the sailing flight of doves.
The least may be the brickdust and explosions.

III. Therefore I meditate, not to despise
What man's whole error has constructed here;
Neither to cry "Repent!" upon this struggle
Or teach the intractable race to sigh my tune.
I have not drunk my fear and shame; yet I
Still must affirm that you uncharitable
Are blessed with my disdain, as I with yours.

        The mind comes to its flowering time
The senses achieve morning
By charity and hope. Let it be known
In the great night and murmur of the age.
This purgatorial city with its glow
Might let a dove fly through, into that later
Radiance and festival the earth promised
When man took up his plow among her stars.

IN THE GLASS

I. RIFLE fire out of the East — a bitter
Range in the red sun, leveler of all
And shadower of men on the low hills

Greening above the mist: blue glacial shadows
Hollow to westward where the faces peer
On surgical terrains lit by the faint fire

Of spring and dawn and war:

Smoke drifting as a frost breath drifting
Home among the orchards: stir, encampments
Clanking with soft metal in the vast

Azure of danger:
                    Hushed on the hot ground
Where one man's crying mouth breaks stones
Leaves, dusty earth, and shuts up soaking:

Flash at eye-lash, and the needle-bright bombers
Borne by scourging savagery of engines
In sensitive chevrons under purest cirrus

Drift and dream on.

II. When night has cast his dreadful shade
And the great sphere inclines
Eastward and weightless, grade by grade
Sacred Arcturus shines.

And cold as starlight through the grove
Where summer's windrows lie
The gliding firefly shines on love
With phosphorescent thigh.

But eastward where vast history wanes
The dust-cloud armies gleam,
And Europe's dark magnetic plains
Glow under nodes of dream,

Whose ether fever's rippling prayer
Breaks on our western sill.
Through all the sighing lands the fair
Sleepers will not be still.

III. The rifle butt falls on the shore
By the quiet path where yesterday's
Immaculate questioners
Tracked down desire. Think, child,
All that is done without remorse
In this sensuous summer dusk
Was dreamed then by the seedy dreamers.
O lakes where the green glaciers sleep,
O mountains fuming cloud,
Be mindful, remember their bondage.

And the red priest that bears his oil
To the still bed in night time
Hears each tragedian weep.
Dear child, who should see paradise,
I'd thee absolve of thy mortality

That flourished from immortal time
Like the cold root and cankered tree
That made Christ's blinding rood.
Or mother within mother — a winding sheet
Stained with rouge and blood.

The vacuum roars in the press rooms,
And the soft announcer's voice clips
Into a beating music.
By rivers, under footlighted cities,
The compact locomotives jostle
Luminous, loud in the night;
The wings of roaring funfighters
Waggle in grey cloud-hung squadrons:
Combustive music, power beyond power,
Rending and rest for the heart.

IV. Caught in the notch of the sights and held there,
Screwed two points for wind: the frozen squirrel
Knocked down, adorable, from the walnut bough.

It was the Winchester won the Indian wars
By bolt action and by force of repetition;
A sweet piece: sweet and hot for the cavalry
After ambrosial Custer's Colt grew cold.

Now rapid as woodpeckers in evening trees
Or riveters in shipyard; fed for percussion
Steel-jacketed decimals out of belts in boxes,
Wickedly weighted, bandy and low slung,
These marvels beat the jungle's yellow eyes.

By night flame splinters from their searching
    muzzles —
Or when you see that dust kicked up, flop down.

Spider-legged lightning dances miles;
While yellow stormcloud and black sighing trees
Flare under his great riding, his fiery veins
Branch to dark earth in thunder.
                            Canned goods
Prepared in one and two ton cylinders
By industrial logic make his strokes look tender.

This theater is everywhere, all the world,
And all the men and women snapshots merely,
Lit by the cold instantaneous street scene.
When wind blows here there's bloody murder done —
Such separation of the cellular form
No ligatures will tie what's torn together.
The quiet earth of God
Spouting the solar gases: smoking and crying
Till comic sirens die in the silent newsreel.

V. The sparrows chirping on the boulevards
And the velvet light on the lawns
In the old provinces.
Carriages covered in linen
And the horses' fetlocks twinkling,
The fine spokes glittering. Clop clop. Creak.
Then tenders of machines, valve readers, skilled
Oilers and handlers of waste, slow moving
Among shining and whining lathes and cutters.

103

"Here was his hand and there his fingers
Lay right over there." Trainmen in mist
Softly waving their lights;
The dusty builders in the stencil of sunlight.

To free those prisoned, defeated in cities:
To make of their many hands one iron pressure:
To unchain and train that power:

Scholars have risen from the world's disorder,
Sleepless when the stars fade, silent
Keepers of history, their bodily will
Geared to the majestic transit of heaven;
Pliant as whips, at ease in multitudes,
Beloved and unloving, responsible.

Though they suckle thin breasts in the South
Or dangle sleigh ropes in the Christmas snow,
All is ordained for this earth's delicate children.
Or is it thus ordained?

Let them not serve abstraction with lies.
The power fails among the unperceptive,
The bitter captains brawl, the pilots rage,
And cities sift toward the streams.
Let their care be constantly at home,
Their marksmanship rare as justice.
Slowly may they learn the earth
In the mastered and peaceful seasons,
The new tongues, the literatures like spring;
Let their rooms be caskets of the sun,
Their rustling hearths at evening
Be theaters to old men's eyes.

SYMPATHY OF PEOPLES

No but come closer. Come a little
Closer. Let the wall-eyed hornyhanded
Panhandler hit you for a dime
Sir and shiver. Snow like this
Drives its pelting shadows over Bremen,
Over sad Louvain and the eastern
Marshes, the black wold. It sighs
Into the cold sea of the north,
That vast contemptuous revery between
Antiquity and you. Turn up your collar,
Pull your hatbrim down. Commune
Briefly with your ignorant heart
For those bewildered raging children
Europe surrenders her old gentry to.

All their eyes turn in the night from
Your fretfulness and forgetfulness,
Your talk; they turn away, friend.
Their eyes dilated with dreams of power
Fix on the image of the mob wet
With blood scaling the gates of order.
Anarchist and incendiary
Caesar bind that brotherhood
To use and crush the civil guard,
Debauch the debauché, level
Tenement and court with soaring
Sideslipping squadrons and hard regiments,
Stripped for the smoking levée of the
Howitzer, thunderstruck under the net.

The great mouth of hunger closes
On swineherd and princess, on the air
Of jongleur and forest bell; Grendel
Swims from the foul deep again.
Deputy, cartelist, academician
Question in haste any plumeless captain
Before the peremptory descent
Of mankind, flattered and proud.
With whitening morning on the waste
You may discern through binoculars
A long line of the shawled and frozen,
Moving yet motionless, as if those
Were populations whom the sun failed
And the malicious moon enchanted
To wander and be still forever
The prey of wolves and bestial mazes.

AUGUSTAN SUITE

I. THAT summer the two godstars in the night
Joined their select shining: Saturn and Jove
Over leaftime and harvest visitant.

At street's end, too, the equatorial star
Gave light at rising, and the round evening moon —
So fortunate in his world was this poor creature.

Leafage and fruit held all his western heart
To husbandry and dust. The smoothing rivers
Dimpled with his sinkers; the blue ponds
Mirrored his pines in their wild quietude.

By lamplight as the climbing summer cooled,
Voices besought him from the savage air:

"Think how unkindness has such history
It clouds the demented planet in the east."

And one said: "I have left my blood with her
On her small dress: all she may have of me."

And many voices. The late summer fragrance
Closed on their fading in the western night,
The broken, the revelatory air
Stoppered and still. Surely those stars shone on.

And men turned to their pleasure or to weep;
But time set onward toward another summer.

II. The sea-crest tossed and running in the rock,
Whirling the grains in its clear troubled liquid,
Leaves to the sun a rim of brine and algae.

If a grey storm should rise it might leave there
Some soaked and bloated mariner, upturned
From avenues where the dim shark whips and courses.

It is not mercy toils upon the capes
Forever, on that swimming stone — the salt
Taste on the steady wind of living ocean,
Too hoary for the watery blood of men;

Nor are they merciful who search its limit
For wispings on the crudded ridge of cloud.

They say: "This diving thing with all its gear
Was given us to be our dangerous room
Where each is necessary." And the others:
"We came from tenements to this sea-light,
From frozen dawns of drunkenness came here
To suffocate or burn. It is all right."

The hairline cuts the center of the image.
The fish glides out among the sheaths of water.

In loneliness the poor hull lifts and showers,
Its merchandise at last distributed.
And the circular sea is perfect as before.

III. When Johnson's uncle wrestled in the ring —
Before young Chatham strode to Parliament —
The Indiamen stood in upon the river.

Those dipping argosies! Blood of the poor
Blackened the pride of two great centuries.
And Arthur Balfour knew the age of ice
Had come and gone and yet would come again.

But reckoned without the mad incendiary.

In our own day we saw on the stately curve
Left by the Regency, or in the tubes,
Nodding, so brightly lit, with evening papers,
That fortunate weariness the world envied —
All indignation exiled to the mines.
And summer novelists with tight umbrellas
Prolonged the sickening Addisonian tone,
Fancier than the mutterings of St. Paul's
Or tenement shade and joy, consumptive breath.

Now the wings brace them in the oxygen stream.
Gull shadows over sea.

                Cloudlight on ocean.
Foamcape spread about headland —
Downward, far westward, remembered.

                        Onset of heaven's
Eastern rack, over continent roaring, a spindrift
Rinsed out of vision.

              Darkness of land in rifts.

IV. Where Easter had her tapers and her lilies,
The grey field officers pace the famous hall,
Their heels deliberately ringing.
With reference to those who died they meditate

Little, but with exactitude and knowledge:
Myriads remain and are not slain and train
For sleepless and calculable combat.
Meanwhile the slow surveying of the frescoes,
The edifices of the grand baroque —
A soldier's earning and a soldier's ease.

"Such sweet liqueurs delight us in this summer!
A cloud like a flower at a lady's ear
Stays sunlit beside evening's Madeleine!
Her perfume, from the first lascivious,
Made us in our forest desire her.

"And ah, now in the night no motor stirs,
But all the city's gardens breathe for us
Unblued and pure their hyacinthine wind.
So was it, maybe, for great Richelieu,
Or in the crystal night of Baudelaire."

The logic of the ganglia, lies and terror
They may this hour forget; here is the world-
City of all the slowly wandering past,
Dark with its tears and love; and here begins
That history they conceive as destiny.

V. In the morning the dew shines on the lawns
At Pasadena, listing to sea and valley:
Freshness cropped by the sun. The fishermen
On vaporous ocean, far out, rising and falling,
Welcome that fire topping the coast range.

This is the land of gold. The fathers fought
Their way in snow and rock, or southwest gales
Below the spouting jut of continent
To claim and thieve her gravelly streams.
Her plains are sweet with Mediterranean harvest,
Starry the naves and foil of her sierras.
Once those alone could run her buffalo surge
Who shipped as seamen from the western islands;
The slim erotic children swim it now.

And are grown intimate with the coastal air,
The mist at morning smoking off the sea,
Or sea-fog pouring on peninsulas.
And have inherited a house of truth
Designed in the great builder's natural heart
For sun's fine ornamenting, for the clear
Mingling of lovely space; and man his measure
Whereby mere shelter became musical.

That they should merit what they know — grow
Straight in some new, forethoughtful courtesy.

VI. The fluid North to which the needle trims,
The fixed star in its tiny ambit, have
No counterpart for general ambition,
So various the sublunary tides of men.
Charity, peace and patience would do well,
Better than empire, were this swarm so manly
Prayer could assuage or humble it. But Learning
May yet be deemed the undiscovered Pole.

Loquere quae decent sanam doctrinam:

Like some great master of Nature, not too mild,
Nor awed by the encircled mystery,
But bearing his fine pressure continually
Toward the gay abnegation that is grace,
The simplifying diligence of honor.
Not love, love is too necessary and dear,
Too usual a crooning, much too rare,
But rather, good instruction and delight.

All things provisional, all absolute:
Conditions, terms and times; power a pit
For passion to beware of; translate that
To the mere mastery that allows respect
For innocent and inscrutable liberty.
So might the humble flourish, so the surgeon's
Violent cut might spare, spare us and save.

COLORADO

Now THE plains come to adore the mountain wall,
Their yellow fields running and bowing like waves
To celebrate in such serene order the fire
And love that bore these stony things. Now fragile
Air, sweet health of a superficial season
Garland a while the majesty of winter.

And I, not long nor with profit hereabouts,
Note merely the blue, the watercolor blue
A descriptive man would like; the rare
And rifted shadowline of trees, the smooth
Peaks too cold for the warm west to redden,
Much, or gild them. They remain sharply vague.

It is so, too, I think, with the remote
Population of memory: they stand above
Our imperceptible journeys and indulgence,
Easily unseen by a simple turn of the head,
Impossible to grasp in contour, always a little
Shifting, and the same. Death has engraved them
Lovely and lofty, and my metaphysic
Smiles to align them here, the shadowy ones
Tinted so faint, yet luminous as gems.

A property of distance. And distance?
A requisite of the just, which is proportion,
Or holy measure, that the sages loved,
Being so fond of stringed instruments and so
Mild: they liked puppies as well as you;

And saw fit, being profound, not to reflect
Chaos unbounded, but to extract therefrom
Numerous order and magnificence.

So at least I interpret the very thin hostile azure
Wherein these stones are dipt, and I imagine
Of time and the great dead, they too
Correctly make a tune with me; let me
Behold by their grave light my minuscule
Part in the swaying and tranquil grandeur here.

POEMS · 1943–1956

for Sarah

PACIFIC

"I AM GREEN under my cloud," the island said,
At dawn in a dim glass on the port side,
Foresail dovebreasted leaning to that bride,
Hesperidean, in her blossoming bed.

Target enlarging, gunned in the needling roar
Until drawn downward under ponderous blood,
We left her rocket-torn perimeter
As the pale brain labored for altitude.

PHYSIS

NOT ART, but craft and cumberment of war
Reduced the wide world to a vector chart,
Hot metal, vapor burning.
                                Thunderheads
Towered about a squadron on a strike,
Aloof, alive, a majesty of forms,
But ghostly, that when cleft were all a mist.

So carnal Nature, ancient manifold,
Would lapse and fade before her violent son
Into a depth of turbulences, charged.

AMPHIBIANS

I. THE CONVOY under a continent of storm
Enters a gloom, a region floored by wind
With fleeces lifted from the dusk of ocean.

Air that was tender in the calms of summer
And touched the shining heads of waves and children
Veers like a runner on the serious sea.

Listen to the sound of the dark
Whistling and groaning: Meet her: the shrouded
    deckhouse
And deck descending sadly toward the blow:

A rumbling, then a burdened surge and frisking
Ramp of enormous water foaming away.

II. A trigger grip easily releasing a brilliant
    vapor,
A fanning plume: see how it licks up smoking
The starved and atrocious seafarer in its fire.

And down hell's terrace in a thicket rent
By the kicking rifle's shot a climber hit
In crablike sacklike slide and puppet's tumble

Dusts his flopping arm.
He must go blind out of the war and bleed
And die to breed again a busy darkness:

Rags of the sunny groin flies' hatching pit.
Be desiccate, O derelict in the sand.

SEAMAN'S LUCK

THE SICK one in a fo'c'sle fevered
And creaking on a sour sea,
In dream conjures a calm landfall,
The morning star in a bay reflected.

Gray and cold, the ocean damp
Blows from the forward hatch in gusts;
The humid engines throb and tramp.
Call Eden death's forethoughtfulness,

Or will the bridge bring out of mists
The lofty land, the cloudy sweet
Fields of the old land, old kingdom?
He dreams he never knew those lawns

Nor, bashful, his embowered home,
The veined leaves dusky in the air,
Nor heart at ease in sighing summer,
His woman cool beside his knee—
The sunset flush upon
Her cheek's classic inclination.

THE SUN in the south ranges a winter heaven
Of crooked sticks and smoke, a silver glare
Low and blinding in the hard cold.
Go down any street: it has long darkened,
Abiding your bleary eye with patience,
Your pity with a crazed forgotten cupola,
Stained by the truths of rain and switch-engines:
A home for the aged. Cut through any yard,
The grey mud when it melts will run gold
Into a morning gutter but soon go black —
The drain of a smelly thaw. Now the frost
Holds, and the winter, and the winter sun,
As a single stranger, ducking against the sting
That blows across lots, comes, and at a corner
Heaves his old overcoat apart, scrabbling
Up from his hip a sticky ball of handkerchief:
Out for an airing on Sunday afternoon.

THE WINTER NIGHT'S DREAM

THE MIND in double gloom detained,
The slow dawn, filling up with snow,
Return me to the dream I feigned
Of some dark life-time long ago.

Whether by dream or feigning true,
In a vast city's drift and throb,
Keeping a bare house known to few
I dwelt to windward of a mob;

And would not sortie in the wind,
But when the wind fell, then I cried
In a low voice to my hunted kind-
red to run for it outside.

And down a causeway hastening home
We came, as from the Peloponnese
Exiles in long cloaks would come
To the sea-lit captain, Pericles,

And saw the marble spaced in air,
Painted against the Ionian,
The Aegean deep of heaven there
In the rational savage city of man —

And, seated high in that place of gold,
The Moirai of the mournful dark
Suburbs where iron traffic rolled
The people tuned to a measured spark.

My heart misgave when I saw this,
And I turned with my fellow shades unseen
From the sweet faithless metropolis
Where in the dream my home had been;

For the cities were the same.
                              I wake
To a world of light where cold twigs push
Fingers of snow at the new snow cake,
And crimson from the clear daybreak
The sun flames in a burning bush.

SOLSTITIUM SAECULARE

WINTER blows on my eaves,
And tall stalks nod in the snow
Pitted by dripping trees.

The strong sun, brought low,
Gives but an evening glare
Through black twigs' to-and-fro

At noon in the cold air.
A rusty windmill grates.
I sit in a Roman chair,

Musing upon Roman fates,
And make my peace with Rome
While the solar fury waits.

I hold my peace at home
And call to my wondering mind
The chaos I came from —

Waste sea and ancient wind
That sailing long I fought,
Unshriven and thin-skinned.

God knows why I perished not,
But made it here by grace
To harbor beyond my thought,

To the stillness of this place.
Here while I live I hold
Young hope in one embrace

With all the ruin of old,
And bless God's will in each;
And bless His word of gold

As far as heart can reach,
Turning the Apostle's page
Or Thomas, who would teach

Peace to the heart's rage.

MISE EN SCENE

THE LAST light muffles itself in cloud and goes
Wildly in silence to the west
Beyond the rough ridge and the pasture snows.

How pale it turns away, like a madman's guest,
Or the queen in the tragedy drawn back
To her luminous height with sickness in her breast.

Leaving us weak as before to murmur "Alack" —
Though here is but Nature turning to night,
Nor angel nor fury glides in the planet's track.

We own no powers in heaven, though well we might
Crave such company of the air
To make majestic our harrowing and our fright.

By what grand eye were these images summoned there?

THE SOLEMN whippoorwill
That sang the dusk away grew still again.
Now from the summer night most still
Moth after moth comes feathery to the pane.

Now we have filled our kitchen with cold fire,
The salamandrine bird of Araby
Refreshed upon his pyre
Had no such incandescence as have we.

Enchanted by that dazzle and driven wild
From the wood, on powdered wings,
So lightly made and of a stuff so mild,
Come the soft beating things.

We see them on the black night, blind with
        love,
Flutter and cling, wings down.
Each one has ermine or satin robes, and bears
        above
A wand and crown.

LIGHTNESS IN AUTUMN

THE RAKE is like a wand or fan,
With bamboo springing in a span
To catch the leaves that I amass
In bushels on the evening grass.

I reckon how the wind behaves
And rake them lightly into waves
And rake the waves upon a pile,
Then stop my raking for a while.

The sun is down, the air is blue,
And soon the fingers will be, too,
But there are children to appease
With ducking in those leafy seas.

So loudly rummaging their bed
On the dry billows of the dead,
They are not warned at four and three
Of natural mortality.

Before their supper they require
A dragon field of yellow fire
To light and toast them in the gloom.
So much for old earth's ashen doom.

SPRING SHADE

THE APRIL winds rise, and the willow whips
Lash one another's green in rinsing light.
The dream eludes the waking finger tips.

Buffets the breakfast pane and flashes white
As a mercury arc the sun in the silver ware.
A screen door slams. Today the May flies bite.

Odor of lilac on the billowing air
Enters the child's room. Robin Red Breast
        grieves
The man of memory in his iron chair.

A girl in watered blue, as he conceives,
And shy from study on the garden grass,
Turned a great page of sunprint and new
        leaves,

Closing the volume. You may leave the class,
The Teacher seemed to say. And he was Dunce.
Now all the colored crayons break, alas,

And all the daffodils blow black at once.

MEDITATION

At Fra Angelico's sepulchre in the
Church of Santa Maria Sopra Minerva

HIS WORKING days were golden: Tuscan light
Vested his little priesthood when he drew;
This funeral dusk would never have come right
In his fresh tempera, but the dusk came true.
His morning angels never knew such cold;
He felt it briefly. When his breath was gone,
One there who worked in stone took his death mould
To cut this that a dim lantern shines on:
The angelic brother, his starved lineaments
Harshly chiselled in the cowl, his eyes
Staring at fearful peace, his formal hands,
Where the rude cape divides, chastened crosswise:
Ancient and homely in the floor at Rome.
Here Pope and prior let the mortal tears come.

THE PAINTER

On bluish inlets bristling
Black in the tall north,
Like violet ghosts risen
The great fish swam forth,
And hoary blooms and submarine
Lightning in the cradling west
Lent summer her virid sheen
For the deep eye's interest.

A fleece on furry nothing,
A web of nightfall grey,
And a leaf tangled, mothing
In a well of yellow day,
Gave him a mile of corner
For a picture like a sea —
The sail and the dream sojourner
Outlined in ivory.

A lank hand had his master
To shear through light like tin
And bitter taste of plaster
When jack boots shook Berlin;
And wine clusters, Venetian,
And Burgundy and France,
Coral and carnelian
Bled white under his glance.

Now shall the man of dust live
And the green man of mould?
The whetted winter rustling

Snows on the Baltic cold,
Where ma'amselle and the trooper
Embraced against the fire
Aflame in the icy pupil;
And art unfleshed desire.

ERRANTRY

THE BABY wades alone across the lawn,
Intrepid, with his golden head upright,
In stubbing steps, as though he rode upon

Two stilts already at a giant's height;
Then down he plunks on his great snowy seat
Of diaper in the ant's land, in the sunlight

Hot on the smudgy toes of both his feet.
Rages of Infancy! How he could cry!
But man's attempt he loves and will repeat,

Surging and teetering, with impassioned eye,
To reach the wildwood lilac shade, and enter
Under the Persian leaves where kittens lie,

Green-eyed, bedizened, at the dappled center.

HISTORY

It is Leviathan, mountain and world,
Yet in its grandeur we perceive
This flutter of the impalpable arriving
Like moths and heartbeats, flakes of snow
Falling on wool, or clouds of thought
Trailing rain in the mind: some old one's dream
Of hauling canvas, or the joy of swording
Hard rascals with a smack — for lordly blood
Circulates tenderly and will seep away;
And the winds blowing across the day
From quarters numberless, going where words go
And songs go, even the holy songs, or where
Leaves, showering, go with the spindling grasses.
Into this mountain shade everything passes.
The slave lays down his bones here and the hero,
Thrown, goes reeling with blinded face;
The long desired opens her scorched armpits.
A mountain; so a gloom and air of ghosts,
But charged with utter light if this is light,
A feathery mass, where this beholding
Shines among lustrous fiddles and codices,
Or dusky angels painted against gold
With lutes across their knees. Magical grain
Bound up in splay sheaves on an evening field,
And a bawling calf butchered — these feed
The curious coil of man. A man, this man,
Bred among lakes and railway cars and smoke,
The salt of childhood on his wintry lips,
His full heart ebbing toward the new tide

Arriving, arriving, in laughter and cries,
Down the chaotic dawn and eastern drift,
Would hail the unforeseen, and celebrate
On the great mountainside those sprites,
Tongues of delight, that may remember him —
The yet unborn, trembling in the same rooms,
Breakfasting before the same grey windows,
Lying, grieving again; yet all beyond him,
Who knew he lived in rough Jehovah's breath,
And burned, a quiet wick in a wild night,
Loving what he beheld and will behold.

POEMS · 1956–1970

for Maria Juliana

TIROLO

Gold on the glen and gloom on the mountain,
High stone dusted with autumn snow;
From windy sky and dusky valley
Summer wanes, and it's time to go.

In the rainy spring, by the soaking meadow,
The coursing glassy streams
Flashed in the day and rushed in the night
With a water-sound under dreams.

The orchards lifted fingers of blossom,
The white clouds lifted up their hands,
And the sun moved like a plowing farmer
Higher and higher on mountain lands.

And tall and purple the meadow clover,
Tender and green grew the climbing vine,
And sweet were the airs of summer, summer,
Warm grass, cattle, and pitch-pine.

Cows in the strong light moved for shadow,
Goats reached up for their bramble fare,
Mowers went swinging down the meadow
And women raked at the teddings there.

Gold on the glen and gloom on the mountain,
High stone dusted with autumn snow;
From windy sky and dusky valley
Summer wanes, and it's time to go.

137

FIGLIO MAGGIORE

Benedict Robert Campion Fitzgerald

TWITCHED in her belly, or he raised a fist,
and came and cried. O red and meager baby,
umbilical, priapic, knobby,
mashed and wrinkled as an old pugilist.

A lyric name he got and a saint's name,
a third stout name from Pa, *cioè Roberto*.
Think of this Christian if you care to
filling his giant napkin without shame.

And soon for happy trilled at goldy leaves
by a summer air. What hours our boy would warble.
You find my doting lines intolerable?
Never was infant such under such eaves.

Behave. "I'm being hayve." With Harpo's grin.
At three he shook his cap and bells, our jester,
or tented him in a souwester
and fragrant slicker to stay in the rain in.

Never (ah!) to inherit that dripping grove,
in a DC–6 he peered at cumulo-cirrus
"trees" on ocean. (Graciously hear us,
lord of that aircraft gaily named I LOVE)

Ligurian fry inquired, "Why is your old man
home all day? What *mestiere* has he?"

"Da notte va fuori a rubare case."
A penman's alibi. Tie it if you can.

Off iodine-scented rock pure undersea,
fronded, astir, awaited our explorer.
Noon. With a tentacled small horror
draped on his tines he swam ashore in glee.

Daemonic lightning, ire of rebellious powers
could rend this patient hunter of the polyp.
Bone-ache from one corrective wallop
disabled the parental hand for hours.

Child of my own rage, rippling in Tuscan speech
through five hard winters' *compiti,* my Benny,
temi, storie, disegni!
What will the next years teach?

JULY IN INDIANA

THE WISPY cuttings lie in rows
        where mowers passed in the heat.
A parching scent enters the nostrils.

Morning barely breathed before
        noon mounted on tiers of maples,
fiery and still. The eye smarts.

Moisture starts on the back of the hand.

Gloss and chrome on burning cars fan out
cobwebby lightning over children
        damp and flushed in the shade.

Over all the back yards, locusts
buzz like little sawmills in the trees,
        or is the song ecstatic? — rising
rising until it gets tired and dies away.

Grass baking, prickling sweat, great blazing tree,
magical shadow and cicada song
        recall
those heroes that in ancient days, reclining
on roots and hummocks, tossing pen-knives,
        delved in earth's cool underworld
and lightly squeezed the black clot from the blade.

Evening came, will come with lucid stillness
            printed by the distinct cricket
and, far off, by the freight cars' coupling clank.

            A warm full moon will rise
out of the mothering dust, out of the dry corn land.

HOSPITAL VISIT

            for A.L.

THIS HARD guy in white jacket and white shoes,
Just coming out, will give me the latest news:
            Pancreatitis complicating diabetes.

Bare to the waist, tangled in tubes, all bone,
With starting eyes, my friend is not alone:
            I gather from his crackling gasp he sees

Whores in the corners, and the Irish nurse
Tells me it has been funnier and worse:
            "Yesterday it was Lady Hamilton, if you please."

CHASSE-NEIGE

for J.L.

BY ROCKING forward on your
toes you allow the heels
of the skis to drift apart

& the points converge sliding
into a right angle into
thousands of faint right

angles engraved by downward
ever-shuffling ski-rules
on the fine stuff of snow

GERMINAL

WITHIN my carapace shriveled and blind,
I wintered in the cold and acrid loam.
I feel a wound now, wet. Something I find
Blading out of my side. What dreams may come
Must give us pause, I hear somewhere behind.
In a slow shift and paroxysm, numb,
I bulge into the sunlight of my kind.
This fantasy or fire I take for home.

AERIAL

INACCURATELY from an old rocking chair
One saw the rivery lands and lifted snows.
Then the Wrights' fabrication and Bleriot's
Annexed the cumulus kingdom of the air.
Helmeted birdmen looped the loop at the Fair
And ranged in later squadrons to impose
On somber towns the tremor of their blows
Or lightning stitches, adding flare on flare.
So much of heaven gained, so much of hell,
Made way for transcendental craft ensuing,
Emissaries not to be disavowed;
But let us pause on thee, sweet Caravel,
Dauphin of jets, in azure halls reviewing
Tall *parfaits* and pudding of whipped cloud.

DUDLEY FITTS

for C.H.F.

THE ORGANIST has closed his instrument
After recessional, and closed his book;
Counterpoint that his fingers undertook
Into the world of light has made ascent.
Airy agilities for perfection spent
Have quieted at last, but not the look
From the musician's eyes that will not brook
A blundering word upon a great event.
Far from New England's leafiness I write
In that land of the old latinity
And golden air to which at length he came,
My master and friend, as to his own birthright.
What farther land he found I hope to see
When by my change our evenings are the same.

SILVER AGE SONG

DROPLET in the western air,
Flashing tremulously fair,

Couching star, this evening shine
On velleities like mine.

Bless all bridals long foregone;
Wake us not this night alone.

Wild beasts in their lairs abide;
Grant us gentle, side by side.

Underground lie grisly men;
Let each swan pair with his pen.

Child of heaven and the sea,
Grace our mortal venery.

AUTUMN BROOK SONG

HERE I dipped, and here my naiad
In her sunny current moving
Rippling took my life away.

Fold your golden arms and sigh
Addio tesoro, goodbye loving,
Goodbye summer where we lay.

145

JULIANA

for T.S.M.

MY DREAM could not have gone the way it has
But for one turning that her touch made known,
And that, and more, has brought me back alone,
Revenant, where I heard her funeral mass.
Here is her churchyard and her church. I pass
Between low walls and cross to find the stone.
Magnolia chalices now overblown
In waxen petals litter the new grass.
At her untended corner nothing stirs.
The headstone, by some buckling of the ground,
Inclines a trifle, in a pensive way
I recklessly, and ill, recall as hers:
Walking half-smiling, in the world she found
More magical and droll than I can say.

METAMORPHOSIS

A BODY made of February rain,
Insipid deliquescence, flat and sane,
Non-alcoholic, chill, perfectly chaste,
Is that by which I feel my own replaced.

PATRUM PROPOSITUM

for W.M.

BEWILDERED in our buying throng,
    What came of it too well we know,
Of Santa Fe and Oregon,
    Of Adams, Jefferson, Monroe.

The Fathers' influences abate;
    And yet they live in the mind's eye,
Their ancient quest and craft of state
    Essences above history,

Elated, practical, and proud —
    As in high air to a small boy,
In August, wagon trains of cloud
    Bear westward over Illinois.

147

TERCETS

IN THE NAME of the father and his world without end
Quiet in being though all things pass away
Whose life is passage whither his will intend,

And of the son whose unseen lightnings play
Through every knitting by knowing each in each,
Pulled in the mind's glass to a burning ray,

And in the like name of that flame of speech
Love made to start upon us in every tongue,
Winged from the zenith and the blue sea's reach,

Holy spirit, high gale when Christ was hung
Breathe on our penury and teach our hands
Largesse of harpers.
                              Great rains move among

The salt-white deserts and cadaverous lands.

GLORIA

CHOIR, angels, and bray, ass:
What *lux,* what *veritas*
Keep we this Christmass?

Only the best we know
Who *ex officio*
Braying or singing go.

EPIPHANY

UNEARTHLY lightning of presage
In any dark day's iron age
May come to lift the hair and bless
Even our tired earthliness,

And sundown bring an age of gold,
Forgèd in faëry, far and old,
An elsewhere and an elfin light,
And kings rise eastward in the night.

JESU, JOY OF MAN'S DESIRING

Chorale from Cantata No. 147, by J. S. Bach,
arranged for piano by Myra Hess

Ivory in her black, and all intent
Upon the mirror of her instrument,
Doubling her beauty to the eye and ear,
My Muse arranged this in a distant year.

I thought my longing then could not abide
The discipline to place me at her side
Whose love and art were joined without defect,
Luxurious touch and sway of intellect.

Korê and lady, Myra, downward glancing
Over the hand that sings to the hand dancing,
Breathe and be present, now the shades grow still.
Sweet air, be figured at your mistress' will.

As he of Brandenburg hummed in his heart,
The tenor and the alto, part by part,
Mounted in joy amid the tranquil choir
To dwell but tenderly on man's desire.

Softly that note fell, for the baby burning
Under the wintry sign of his sojourning,
The westward star, lay upon Eden's breast
Where husbandman and hunter seek to rest.

So voices woke from every falling voice,
Bidding the Gentile and the Jew rejoice,

With all that generations may conceive,
In Miriam, who is the grace of Eve.

Had she not borne the seed of the Lord God
To ripen in her splendid belly's pod?
And who but sages of the fragrant East
Dared his epiphany, adorned the feast?

And how but in the Cyprian's tongue went round
The tidings of great joy upon that ground
And peaceful glory promised in the air?
Holy became the rose our bodies bear.

So ran the Kapellmeister's hymn unending,
So dreamed the maiden on his word attending,
So, as I cherished her in my degree,
The page of ancient music fell to me.

Now life has turned and all seems far and late,
Knowing what dark declensions I await,
I hold these truthful and am not beguiled:
The girl, the singing, and the Christmas child.

METAPHYSICAL

In festo Christi Regis

THE LEVEL slope of colored sea
Rises degree upon degree
To hide the brazen ball of sun.
Ponderous is the planet side,
And nothing here but heart can slide,
And nothing but the day is done.

Glory the heavens here declare
Heavens in gloom deny elsewhere.
The jackal and the gaping shark
Possess the shambles of the night.
As upward eyries take the light
The downward longitudes are dark.

Eyes on the telluric rim
In tangent angles peering dim
Find shape and hour dark or down.
But centered lordship knows the art
Of bearing so toward every part
The studded sphere becomes his crown.

Rays of his mercy are besought
To magnetize my speck of thought.
Elated let the evening fall,
Abysmal be the golden day;
The ravaged carcass far away
Be supple in the life of all.

MATINS IN AN OLD MEASURE

SILKEN cloud, be parasol:
Let the shade of summer fall;
Tinge the blue air deeper blue;
Cobweb, keep your bead of dew.
Morning, morning, by the Mass,
Veil your burning, gently pass.
Under the green, leafy hill,
Ruffling stream, run dark and still,
And still your tremor, butterflies,
While this nymph, with downcast eyes
Over nape and shoulder bare
Slowly braids her burnished hair.

A NATIVITY FOR 1965

REGARD this jewel case in deadly light
Sprung to emit our *poupée* on his cord.
Issue, big blind helmed head! Against his fright
Rampant, our little man goes overboard.
Goes overboard for us. Grand at that height
The wrinkled world and all it's rolling toward.
So bless this parturition while you write,
And as in every other praise the Lord.

DISPOSTO A SALIRE

HAVING preferred what it prefers,
Weightless the fiery mind goes to and fro
Through all the numbered universe,

And free of earth? So fasting lovers are
Who walk in courts of afterglow
To the receptions of the evening star.

A LIKENESS

In festo Corporis Christi

OUR FATE we knew, but could not comprehend,
Though what long thought could hold into the light
Some late Aegeans made less recondite
By inquiry and discourse, friend to friend.
Still we were lonely, till our great godsend
When the invisible took his creature's plight
Of being incarnate, heart-beat day and night
And a mute ignominy at the end.
Now what's the upshot of his passion play
If not our quaint *remedium,* barely sung
Or guessed at by the noble wit of Greece:
All touching things are formed to pass away,
Like his fine wafer breaking on the tongue,
And by this perishing Being has increase.

SELECTED TRANSLATIONS

A PASSAGE FROM HOMER'S ILIAD

THEN on the perilous open ground of war,
in brave expectancy, they lay all night
while many campfires burned. As when in heaven
principal stars shine out around the moon
when the night sky is limpid, with no wind,
and all the look-out points, headland, and mountain
clearings are distinctly seen, as though
pure space had broken through, downward from heaven,
and all the stars are out, and in his heart
the shepherd sings: just so from ships to river
shone before Ilion the Trojan fires.
There were a thousand burning in the plain,
and round each one lay fifty men in firelight.
Horses champed white barley, near the chariots,
waiting for Dawn to mount her lovely chair.

(Book VIII, lines 553–565)

A CHORUS FROM
SOPHOCLES' OEDIPUS REX

ALAS for the seed of men.

What measure shall I give these generations
That breathe on the void and are void
And exist and do not exist?

Who bears more weight of joy
Than mass of sunlight shifting in images,
Or who shall make his thought stay on
That down time drifts away?

Your splendour is all fallen.

O naked brow of wrath and tears,
O change of Oedipus!
I who saw your days call no man blest —
Your great days like ghosts gone.

That mind was a strong bow.

Deep, how deep you drew it then, hard archer,
At a dim fearful range,
And brought dear glory down!

You overcame the stranger —
The virgin with her hooking lion claws —
And though death sang, stood like a tower
To make pale Thebes take heart.

Fortress against our sorrow!

Divine king, giver of laws,
Majestic Oedipus!
No prince in Thebes had ever such renown,
No prince won such grace of power.

And now of all men ever known
Most pitiful is this man's story:
His fortunes are most changed, his state
Fallen to a low slave's
Ground under bitter fate.

O Oedipus, most royal one!
The great door that expelled you to the light
Gave at night — ah, gave night to your glory:
As to the father, to the fathering son.

All understood too late.

How could that queen whom Laïos won,
The garden that he harrowed at his height,
Be silent when that act was done?

But all eyes fail before time's eye,
All actions come to justice there.
Though never willed, though far down the deep past,
Your bed, your dread sirings,
Are brought to book at last.

Child by Laïos doomed to die,
Then doomed to lose that fortunate small death,
Would God you never took breath in this air
That with my wailing lips I take to cry:

For I weep the world's outcast.

Blind I was, and can not tell why;
Asleep, for you had given ease of breath;
A fool, while the false years went by.

KALLIMAKHOS' TO A LYRIC POET

SOMEONE spoke about
the way you went
Hêrakleitos it
brought me to tears

and I remembered
how many a time we two
talking together saw
the sun down to his bed

odd now to think of you
Halikarnassian friend
as ashes long ago

these songs of yours though
are alive still
nightingales
        on them
Death grasping for everyone
will never lay a hand

PASSAGES FROM
VIRGIL'S FIRST GEORGIC

I. UNTIL Jove let it be, no colonist
Mastered the wild earth; no land was marked,
None parceled out or shared; but everyone
Looked for his living in the common wold.

And Jove gave poison to the blacksnakes, and
Made the wolves ravage, made the ocean roll,
Knocked honey from the leaves, took fire away —
So man might beat out various inventions
By reasoning and art.
                              First he chipped fire
Out of the veins of flint where it was hidden;
Then rivers felt his skiffs of the light alder;
Then sailors counted up the stars and named them:
Pleiades, Hyades, and the Pole Star;
Then were discovered ways to take wild things.
In snares, or hunt them with the circling pack;
And how to whip a stream with casting nets,
Or draw the deep-sea fisherman's cordage up;
And then the use of steel and the shrieking saw;
Then various crafts. All things were overcome
By labor and by force of bitter need.

II. Even when your threshing floor is leveled
By the big roller, smoothed and packed by hand
With potter's clay, so that it will not crack,
There are still nuisances. The tiny mouse
Locates his house and granary underground,

162

Or the blind mole tunnels his dark chamber;
The toad, too, and all monsters of the earth,
Besides those plunderers of the grain, the weevil
And frantic ant, scared of a poor old age.

Let me speak then, too, of the farmer's weapons:
The heavy oaken plow and the plowshare,
The slowly rolling carts of Demeter,
The threshing machine, the sledge,
    the weighted mattock,
The withe baskets, the cheap furniture,
The harrow and the magic winnowing fan —
All that your foresight makes provision of,
If you still favor the divine countryside.

III. Moreover, like men tempted by the straits
In ships borne homeward through the blowing sea,
We too must reckon on Arcturus star,
The days of luminous Draco and the Kids.
When Libra makes the hours of sleep and daylight
Equal, dividing the world, half light, half dark,
Then drive the team, and sow the field with barley,
Even under intractable winter's rain.
But Spring is the time to sow your beans and clover,
When shining Taurus opens the year with his golden
Horns, and the Dog's averted star declines;
For greater harvests of your wheat and spelt,
Let first the Pleiades and Hyades be hid
And Ariadne's diadem go down.
The golden sun rules the great firmament

Through the twelve constellations, and the world
Is measured out in certain parts, and heaven
By five great zones is taken up entire:
One glowing with sundazzle and fierce heat;
And far away on either side the arctics,
Frozen with ice and rain, cerulean;
And, in between, two zones for sick mankind:
Through each of these a slanting path is cut
Where pass in line the zodiacal stars.

Northward the steep world rises to Scythia
And south of Libya descends, where black
Styx and the lowest of the dead look on.
In the north sky the Snake glides like a river
Winding about the Great and Little Bear —
Those stars that fear forever the touch of ocean;
Southward they say profound Night, mother of Furies,
Sits tight-lipped among the crowding shades,
Or thence Aurora draws the daylight back;
And where the East exhales the yellow morning,
Reddening evening lights her stars at last.

IV. As for the winter, when the freezing rains
Confine the farmer, he may employ himself
In preparations for serener seasons.
The plowman beats the plowshare on the forge,
Or makes his vats of tree-trunks hollowed out,
Brands his cattle, numbers his piles of grain,
Sharpens fence posts or pitchforks, prepares
Umbrian trellises for the slow vine.

'Then you may weave the baskets of bramble twigs
Or dip your bleating flock in the clean stream.
Often the farmer loads his little mule
With olive oil or apples, and brings home
A grindstone or a block of pitch from market.

And some will stay up late beside the fire
On winter nights, whittling torches, while
The housewife runs the shuttle through the loom
And comforts the long labor with her singing;
Or at the stove she simmers the new wine,
Skimming the froth with leaves. Oh idle time!
In that hale season, all their worries past,
Farmers arrange convivialities —
As after laden ships have reached home port,
The happy sailors load the prow with garlands.
Then is the time to gather acorns and
Laurel berries and the bloodred myrtle,
To lay your traps for cranes and snares for buck,
To hit the fallow deer with twisted slingshots,
And track the long-eared hare —
When snow is deep, and ice is on the rivers.

V. What of the humors and the ways of Autumn?

Just when the farmer wished to reap his yellow
Fields, and thresh his grain,
I have often seen all the winds make war,
Flattening the stout crops from the very roots;
And in the black whirlwind

Carrying off the ears and the light straw.
And often mighty phalanxes of rain
Marched out of heaven, as the clouds
Rolled up from the sea the detestable tempest;
Then the steep aether thundered, and the deluge
Soaked the crops, filled ditches, made the rivers
Rise and roar and seethe in their spuming beds.

The Father himself in the mid stormy night
Lets the lightning go, at whose downstroke
Enormous earth quivers, wild things flee,
And fear abases the prone hearts of men —
As Jove splits Athos with his firebolt
Or Rhodopê or the Ceraunian ridge.
The southwind wails in sheets of rain,
And under that great wind the groves
Lament, and the long breast of the shore is shaken.

If you dislike to be so caught, mark well
The moon's phases and the weather signs;
Notice where Saturn's frigid star retires,
Mercury's wanderings over heaven; and revere
Especially, the gods. Offer to Ceres
Annual sacrifice and annual worship
In the first fair weather of the spring,
So may your sheep grow fat and your vines fruitful,
Your sleep sweet and your mountains full of shade.
Let all the country folk come to adore her,
And offer her libations of milk and wine;
Conduct the sacrificial lamb three times
Around the ripe field, in processional,

166

With all your chorus singing out to Ceres;
And let no man lay scythe against his grain
Unless he first bind oakleaves on his head
And make his little dance, and sing to her.

VI. When shall we herd the cattle to the stables?

The wind, say, rises without intermission;
The sea gets choppy and the swell increases;
The dry crash of boughs is heard on hills;
The long sound of the surf becomes a tumult;
The gusts become more frequent in the grove;
The waves begin to fight against the keels;
From far at sea the gulls fly shoreward crying;
The heron leaves his favorite marsh and soars
Over the high cloud. Then you will see
Beyond thin skimrack, shooting stars
Falling, the long pale tracks behind them
Whitening through the darkness of the night;
And you'll see straw and fallen leaves blowing.
But when it thunders in rough Boreas' quarter,
When east and west it thunders — every sailor
Furls his dripping sail.

A storm should never catch you unprepared.
Aerial cranes take flight before its rising,
The restless heifer with dilated nostrils
Sniffs the air; the squeaking hirondelle
Flits round and round the lake, and frogs,

Inveterate in their mud, croak a chorale.
And too the ant, more frantic in his gallery,
Trundles his eggs out from their hiding place;
The rainbow, cloud imbiber, may be seen;
And crows go cawing from the pasture
In a harsh throng of crepitating wings;
The jeering jay gives out his yell for rain
And takes a walk by himself on the dry sand.
Stormwise, the various sea-fowl, and such birds
As grub the sweet Swan River in Asia,
May be observed dousing themselves and diving
Or riding on the water, as if they wished —
What odd exhilaration — to bathe themselves.

VII. After a storm, clear weather and continuing
Sunny days may likewise be foretold:
By the sharp twinkle of the stars, the moon
Rising to face her brother's rays by day;
No tenuous fleeces blowing in the sky,
No halcyons, sea favorites, on the shore
Stretching out their wings in tepid sunlight;
But mists go lower and lie on the fields,
The owl, observing sundown from his perch,
Modulates his meaningless melancholy.
Aloft in crystal air the sparrow hawk
Chases his prey; and as she flits aside
The fierce hawk follows screaming on the wind,
And as he swoops, she flits aside again.
With funereal contractions of the windpipe
The crows produce their caws, three at a time,

And in their high nests, pleased at I know not what,
Noise it among themselves: no doubt rejoicing
To see their little brood after the storm,
But not, I think, by reason of divine
Insight or superior grasp of things.

VIII. But if you carefully watch the rapid sun
And the moon following, a fair night's snare
Never deceives you as to next day's weather.
When the new moon collects a rim of light,
If that bow be obscured with a dark vapor,
Then a great tempest is in preparation;
If it be blushing like a virgin's cheek,
There will be wind; wind makes Diana blush;
If on the fourth night (most significant)
She goes pure and unclouded through the sky,
All that day and the following days will be,
For one full month, exempt from rain and wind.
The sun, too, rising and setting in the waves,
Will give you weather signs, trustworthy ones
Whether at morning or when stars come out.
A mackerel sky over the east at sunrise
Means look out for squalls, a gale is coming,
Unfavorable to trees and plants and flocks.
Or when through denser strata the sun's rays
Break out dimly, or Aurora rises
Pale from Tithonus' crocus-colored chamber,
Alas, the vine-leaf will not shield the cluster
In the hubbub of roof-pattering bitter hail.

It will be well to notice sunset, too,
For the sun's visage then has various colors;
Bluish and dark means rain; if it be fiery
That means an East wind; if it be dappled
And mixed with red gold light, then you will see
Wind and rain in commotion everywhere.
Nobody can advise me, on that night,
To cast off hawsers and put out to sea.
But if the next day passes and the sunset
Then be clear, you need not fear the weather:
A bright Norther will sway the forest trees.

IX. Last, what the late dusk brings, and whence
        the fair
Clouds are blown, and secrets of the Southwind
You may learn from the sun, whose prophecies
No man denies, seeing black insurrections,
Treacheries, and wars are told by him.

When Caesar died, the great sun pitied Rome,
So veiling his bright head, the godless time
Trembled in fear of everlasting night;
And then were portents given of earth and ocean,
Vile dogs upon the roads, and hideous
Strange birds, and Aetna quaking, and her fires
Bursting to overflow the Cyclops' fields
With flames whirled in the air and melted stones.
Thunder of war was heard in Germany
From south to north, shaking the granite Alps;
And a voice also through the silent groves

Piercing; and apparitions wondrous pale
Were seen in dead of night. Then cattle spoke
(O horror!), streams stood still, the earth cracked open
And tears sprang even from the temple bronze.
The Po, monarch of rivers, on his back
Spuming whole forests, raced through the lowland
    plains
And bore off pens and herds; and then continually
The viscera of beasts were thick with evil,
Blood trickled from the springs; tall towns at night
Re-echoed to the wolf-pack's shivering howl;
And never from pure heaven have there fallen
So many fires, nor baleful comets burned.
It seemed that once again the Roman lines,
Alike in arms, would fight at Philippi;
And heaven permitted those Thessalian fields
To be enriched again with blood of ours.
Some future day, perhaps, in that country,
A farmer with his plow will turn the ground,
And find the javelins eaten thin with rust,
Or knock the empty helmets with his mattock
And wonder, digging up those ancient bones.

Paternal gods! Ancestors! Mother Vesta!
You that guard Tiber and the Palatine!
Now that long century is overthrown,
Let not this young man fail to give us peace!
Long enough beneath your rule, O Caesar,
Heaven has hated us and all those triumphs
Where justice was thrown down — so many wars,
So many kinds of wickedness! No honor

Rendered the plow, but the fields gone to ruin,
The country-folk made homeless, and their scythes
Beaten to straight swords on the blowing forge!
War from the Euphrates to Germany;
Ruptured engagements, violence of nations,
And impious Mars raging the whole world over —
As when a four-horsed chariot rears away
Plunging from the barrier, and runs wild,
Heedless of the reins or the charioteer.

CATULLUS' FAREWELL (XI)

FURIUS and Aurelius, aides to Catullus,
Whether he penetrate the ultimate Indies
Where the rolling surf on the shores of morning
    Beats and again beats:

Or in the land of bedouin, the soft Arabs,
Or Parthians, the ungentlemanly archers,
Or where the Nile with seven similar streamlets
    Colors the clear sea;

Or if he cross the loftier Alpine passes
And view the monuments of almighty Caesar,
The Rhine, and France, and even those remotest
    Shuddersome British —

Friends, prepared for all of these, whatever
Province the celestial ones may wish me —
Take a little bulletin to my mistress,
    Unpleasantly worded:

Let her live and thrive with her fornicators
Of whom she hugs three hundred in an evening,
With no true love for any, leaving them broken-
    Winded the same way.

She need not, as in the old days, look for my love.
By her own fault it died, like a fallen flower
At the field's edge, after the passing harrow
    Touched it and left it.

CATULLUS' CI

By STRANGERS' coasts and waters, many days at sea,
　　I came here for the rites of your unworlding,
Bringing for you, the dead, these last gifts of the living
　　And my words — vain sounds for the man of dust.
　　　Alas, my brother,
You have been taken from me. You have been taken
　　from me,
　　By cold chance turned a shadow, and my pain.
Here are the foods of the old ceremony, appointed
　　Long ago for the starvelings under earth:
Take them: your brother's tears have made them wet;
　　and take
　　Into eternity my hail and my farewell.

THE YOUNG men come less often — isn't it so? —
To rap at midnight on your fastened window;
Much less often. How do you sleep these days?

There was a time your door gave with proficiency
On easy hinges; now it seems apter at being shut.
I do not think you hear many lovers moaning

"Lydia, how can you sleep?"
"Lydia, the night is so long!"
"Oh, Lydia, I'm dying for you!"

No. The time is coming when *you* will moan
And cry to scornful men from an alley corner
In the dark of the moon when the wind's in a
    passion

With lust that would drive a mare wild
Raging in your ulcerous old viscera.
You'll be alone and burning then

To think how happy boys take their delight
In fresh and tender buds, the blush of myrtle,
Consigning dry leaves to the winter sea.

MEN AND brothers, who after us shall be,
Let not your hearts too hard against us grow,
For if on us poor men you take pity,
God will be merciful to you also.
You see us, five or six, hung in a row,
That flesh we too much fattened long ago
Now tattered, eaten off, a rotten dough;
And we, the bones, are growing pulverous.
Our wretchedness let no one laugh to see,
But pray God's mercy upon all of us.

If brother men you are, you need not be
Scornful of us, though Justice as I know
Cut short our lives. You know as well as we,
All men cannot be steady here below.
Forgive us, since we are transported so
To Mary's son, to kneel at his elbow,
And never may his fount of grace run low,
From thunderclap of Hell preserving us.
We are dead now, and mind no misery,
Yet pray God's mercy upon all of us.

The rain has drubbed us in his cold laundry,
The sun has parched us blacker than a crow,
And kites have made each eye a cavity
And torn out beards and eyebrows even so.
There is no resting place where we may go,
But here or there, just as the wind may blow,
We dangle at his pleasure to and fro,

Pocked more by birds than thimble surfaces.
Be not therefore of our fraternity,
But pray God's mercy upon all of us.

Prince Jesus, who hath all in mastery,
Over us let not Hell gain sovereignty,
For of it we are no way curious.
Brothers, see nothing here for mockery,
But pray God's mercy upon all of us.

A PASSAGE FROM
VALERY'S NARCISSUS CANTATA

Nymph:

BE, THEN! . . . What has Narcissus done for you
But make you lose your reason? Break his gaze;
Turn your mild eyes from darkening water's hue;
See treason in fair evening's fallen blaze,
Ruins of day, mighty transfigurings,
Ashes of gold shed on the form of things,
The sun's whole pride gone down to petalings,
    Rose pink on distant ways. . .
Fades now your love beneath funereal boughs.
Your brimming fountain, as the dusk allows,
Begins to view the treasures of the night,
Faint fires that announce, on the waste height,
The Universe of terrifying Number. . . .
Newborn abyss, more velvety than somber,
Rich in desires as in her diamonds,
With dusky perfumes that no dreamer shuns,
Enchanted languors, luxuries of slumber
Where lovers come to rest, the dovelike ones.
Unbosoming to the warm night and the stars
My sister naiads let their water jars
Weep chilly tears, a-trickle through pale fingers,
Murmuring of virginity that lingers
Into eternity, all unrelieved.
Narcissus, mortal never yet conceived
The meaning of despair when death's denied.
You that can perish, rage not to abide;
A measured rigor is your mortal lot:

Flesh will be done with ills when flesh is not.
But we, we are unending, always *I*. . .
My heart is yours forever; it will not die.
If only this vague hour, dissolving all,
Could bring a sigh when my entreaties fall,
You would be spared a flower's destiny. . . .
Have you not drunk your dream, that misery?
Do you not hear the tremor of the wood?
Come. . . yield your fruitless grace of solitude,
Yield now to me: the time for hate is past;
O leave Narcissus; be seduced at last. . . .

Narcissus:
Alone I lived, alone let me succumb.

Nymph:
If you must die, then let me be your tomb.
Come lose your sight upon my breast, hide here
From your own pride and Heaven's word of fear. . .

Narcissus:
Nymph, no. . . Nymph, no. . . I cannot give consent
        To this design to set me free.
        If Heaven decree a cruelty,
Let Heaven see to the crime's accomplishment. . . .
Narcissus cannot sigh, will never sigh
        Of true love to another one;
        To the black oath he must reply
        His love is for his love alone
        Whom alien eyes may never cheat:

He fears betrayal to the bone,
And hearts with variable beat. . .
But listen, perilously sweet:

O quivering, slender, dear
Divine girl of the wood,
I do not loathe to hear
Your voice in solitude,
Nor loathe your loveliness;
Only when lashes fill
In bright distress,
You are more lovely still. . .

Vainly in the welkin's court
The Lords of Azure, cold with fate,
Cut Narcissus' lifetime short,
His pride being inviolate.
Vain their edicts fall in thunder,
Vain his dissolution, under
Frail appearance of a flower;
Destiny may still relent
If you weep to breathe my scent,
My sweet shade, immortal power. . . .

Farewell, my Soul, now one must turn to sleep:
Time is no more for noble form to keep
One force, one presence in continual change. . .
Body, Fair Idol of the Watery Glass,
Here is the last day of the days that pass
With brief endurance of the pure and strange. . . .

He disappears.

On MUSIC drawn away, a sea-borne mariner,
   Star over bowsprit pale,
Beneath a roof of mist or depths of lucid air
   I put out under sail;

Breastbone my steady bow and lungs full, running free
   Before a following gale,
I ride the rolling back and mass of every sea
   By Night wrapt in her veil;

All passions and all joys that vessels undergo
   Tremble alike in me;
Fair winds or waves in havoc when the tempests blow

   On the enormous sea
Rock me, and level calms come silvering sea and air,
   A glass for my despair.

7

"AND THUS, high seated, gathering at last the pieces of a wider fabric, we assemble around us all this great terrestrial fact.

Behind us, down there on the slope of the year, the whole earth in straight folds and from all sides drawn in, like the ample cloak of a shepherd knotted up to the chin. . .

(Must we — for the Ocean of things lays siege to us — cover forehead and face? As on the highest headland, under the storm, the man of a great dream may be seen burying his head in a sack to converse with his god?)

. . .And over our shoulder, from this summit, we hear the incessant dripping of the whole world new risen out of the waters.

It is the earth, on all sides, weaving its tawny wool like hemp of byssus from the sea; and the procession, on the far plains, of those great May-blue shadows that lead the herds of heaven so silently over the earth. . .

Irreproachable your chronicle, O earth, to the Censor's eye! We are herdsmen of the future, and all the great Devonian night does not suffice to sustain our praise. . . Are we, ah, are we? — or were we ever — in all that?

★

. . .And all that came to us for good, came to us for ill: the earth moving in its age and its lofty idiom — formation of folds and overfolds, displacements toward the West and endless shifting of watercourses, and on tiered layers like sand-bars at tide-mouth, like unfurlings of surf, the incessant advance of a lip of clay . . .

O memorable face of the Earth, let a cry be heard for you, last come in our praises! Love hardened your wild berries, O earth more wrinkled than sorrows of the Moors! O memory, in man's heart, of the lost kingdom!

The Sky to Westward robes itself like a Caliph, the earth bathes its vines in the red of bauxite, and man bathes in the wine of night: the cooper before his casks, the smith before his forge, and the waggoner bent over the stone trough of the fountains.

Honour to the basins where we drink! The tanneries are places of offering and dogs are smeared with blood from the butcher's waste; but for the dream of our nights, the cutters of bark from the cork-tree have bared a richer tone and darker, colour of a Moor's head.

. . .O memory, take thought for your roses of salt. The great rose of evening lodges a star on its breast like a golden beetle. Beyond the legends of sleep, this pledge to man under his burden of stars!

Great age, you form this praise. The women rise on the plain and march with long steps toward the red copper of existence.

This way has passed the horde of Centuries!

8

. . . Great age, behold us — and our mortal strides toward the issue. Enough of garnering, it is time to air the harvest and honour the threshing floor.

Tomorrow, the great raiding thunderstorms, and the lightning at work. . . The caduceus of the sky descends to mark the earth with its sign. The alliance is sealed.

Ah! may an *élite* also rise, of very tall trees on the earth, like a tribe of great souls that shall hold us of their council. . . And let the severity of evening descend, with avowal of its tenderness, on the roads of burning stone, roads lit with lavender. . .

A quivering then, on the highest stem sticky with amber, of the highest leaf half-detached on its ivory claw.

And our actions dwindle far off in their orchards of lightning. . .

It is for others to build, amid the schist and the lava. For others to raise the marbles in the city.

For us, already, a song of higher adventure. The road traced by a new hand, and fires carried from crest to crest. . .

And these are no weaving songs for the women's quarters, nor fireside songs like 'Queen of Hungary songs' for the shucking of red corn on the rusted blades of old family rapiers,

But a graver song, of another steel, like a song of honour and great age and a song of the Master, alone in the evening, forging his way, before the hearthfire

— pride of the soul before the soul and pride of soul growing to greatness in the great blue sword.

Already our thoughts rise in the night like nomad chieftains of the big tents who walk before daybreak toward a red sky, carrying their saddles on their left shoulders.

Behold the places we leave. The fruits of the soil are beneath our walls, the waters of the sky in our cisterns, and the great millstones of porphyry rest on the sand.

The offering, O night, where to bring it? and the praise, to whom entrust it? . . . We raise, with arms outstretched, on the flat of our hands, like a hatching of nascent wings, this darkened heart of a man where hunger was, and ardour, and so much love unrevealed. . .

Listen, O night, in the deserted courtyards and under the solitary arches, amid the holy ruins and the crumbling of old termite hills, hear the great sovereign footfalls of the soul without a lair,

Like a wild beast prowling a pavement of bronze.

★

Great age, behold us. Take the measure of man's heart."

NEITHER the intimacy of your forehead, fair as
    a feast-day,
Nor the favour of your body, still mysterious,
    reserved and childlike,
Nor what comes to me of your life, settling in words
    or silence,
Will be a grace so provocative of thoughts
As the sight of your sleep, enfolded
In the vigil of my covetous arms.
Virgin again, miraculously, by the absolving power
    of Sleep,
Quiet and luminous like some happy thing recovered
    by memory,
You will deed to me that shore of your life
    that you yourself do not own.
Cast up into silence,
I shall discern that ultimate beach of your being
And see you for the first time as, perhaps,
God must see you,
The fiction of Time destroyed,
    Free from love, from me.

· INDEX ·
TITLES AND FIRST LINES

INDEX

189